PC Music Handbook
Second edition

Brian Heywood and Roger Evan

GW00597309

PC Publishing

PC Publishing
Export House
130 Vale Road
Tonbridge
Kent TN9 1SP
UK

Tel 01732 770893
Fax 01732 770268
e-mail pcp@cix.compulink.co.uk

First published 1991
Second edition 1996

© PC Publishing

ISBN 1 870775 42 2

British Library Cataloguing in Publication Data

A catalogue record for this book is available from the British Library

Printed and bound in Great Britain by Bell & Bain, Glasgow

Foreword

The unprecedented advances in the field of electronic music over the last decade have left us with today's rich diversity of computer music systems and technology. Left in the wake, however, is a legacy of inscrutable acronyms and techno-speak that many still find a barrier when using their PC for music. It is not so very long ago that books on this subject were few and far between, with would-be exponents having to glean their knowledge from a combination of woeful manufacturers' documentation and bitter experience! Now, however, the newcomer is confronted with an almost bewildering array of titles, and the problem is rather one of making the right choice – a choice all too often between shallow oversimplification or the dry, 'textbook' style with inadequate depth of explanation.

In *PC Music Handbook* the authors have compiled a wealth of practical information and invaluable insight, in a work which achieves the rare feat of being able to serve both as reference book and tutorial guide. Their uncondescending style is backed up by an unusually broad knowledge of the field, whilst the book's logical organisation helps you sort the essential information from the 'optional extras'.

Covering everything from basic principles through to real world examples of gettting systems to work together, and rounded off with exhaustive appendices and glossary, this book is an invaluable fund of information, and one you will want to refer to over and over again.

Dave Lockwood
Editor, *Audio Media* magazine

Preface

Since the first edition of the PC Music Handbook, the look and feel of the PC has been revolutionised. The almost universal acceptance of Windows 3 as the preferred 'user interface' for the PC has sounded a death knell for the traditional MS-DOS command line interface, to the point where Windows and PC are becoming synonymous. This process has now reached its culmination with the subsuming of DOS into the Windows operating environment with the release of Windows 95™ – which is billed as a 'full blown' operating system.

In terms of the musical uses of the PC, Windows 3.1 ushered in its own particular revolution in a number of ways. On the technical side, the incorporation of MIDI and digital audio into the operating system meant that music applications are no longer chained to the obsolescent Roland MPU-401 'standard' for talking to external musical devices, which in turn has caused a small explosion in the numbers of different MIDI interfaces available for the PC.

On a more abstract level, the implicit enforcement of a common graphical user interface (or GUI) that using Windows entails has meant that a lot of the quirkiness of the various software packages has disappeared. This tendency is not universal, especially with music applications that have been transferred (or 'ported') from other computing platforms such as the Apple Macintosh™ or Atari ST. Despite this however, there is still enough freedom for creative software authors to 'improve' on the standard Windows way of doing things.

The major advantage of this standardisation in the way computer applications interact with the user is that it cuts down the time it takes to learn how to use a package. This means that if you are familiar with one Windows application, then you are halfway down the path of learning any new software package, and this of course applies to music applications as much as it does to word processors and spreadsheets.

The hardware development of the PC still goes on apace, with ever more powerful processors, cheaper mass storage and better display devices. The concentration on multimedia also has spin-offs that directly or indirectly help the computer musician. And as always, prices keep tumbling as new technologies reduce manufacturing costs and the apparently insatiable demand from the business world allow the economies of scale to take full play.

So whether you are a musician or audio professional interested in taking full advantage of the technology, or you simply want to give vent to your creative urges in your spare time, then the PC is a good choice. It's not the only choice, but it does give a cost effective way of getting into computer based music and audio.

Brian Heywood and Roger Evan

Contents

Introduction to the PC and music

Personal computers and computer music systems have been around for over two decades now. Both started from fairly inauspicious beginnings, and from being expensive and not particularly effective toys they have grown into professional tools. The developments in musical applications have mirrored the growth of the PC market for a number of reasons, the most obvious is that as PCs became more powerful the possibilities for music became more diverse. Another reason is that developments in sound synthesis and particularly the almost universal adoption of the Musical Instrument Digital Interface (MIDI) by electronic instrument manufacturers has meant that the actual burden of producing high quality sound has been removed from the computer.

Latterly, the increase in power of the PC and the subsequent introduction of multimedia aspects to the PC, particularly digital audio facilities, has meant that the entire recording process can be encompassed by the PC. This ability to mix MIDI and digital audio on the same computing platform means that the PC has become a complete solution for the computer musician. With MIDI giving access to tone colours not normally available outside a major recording studio (strings, brass etc.) and the ability to record voice and acoustic instruments to the PC's hard disk we are approaching a revolution in personal sound production in the same way that Desk Top Publishing (DTP) revolutionised document production.

This combination of technology and art has also produced a culture of computer programmers and musicians dedicated to pushing back the frontiers of music technology. Hence, a very wide range of

music and audio applications – from high quality music scoring programs, to performance, teaching and recording systems have been
developed specifically for the PC. This probably would never have
occurred if the only tangible result of the software had been a few
semi-musical bleeps or reams of computer printout.

So we stand on the threshold of the Desk Top Audio (DTA) revolution, which will take the bulk of music making out of the large studio
into the smaller facility – or even into the musician's front room. The
'music business' is in the throes of trying to come to terms with the
changes, but must adapt to survive in the new environment – just as
the large computer manufacturers had to adapt in the face of the personal computing revolution – or go bust.

What about the PC?

Despite the perceived business bias of the IBM PC, it has been
around since near the beginning of the micro-computer revolution, pre-
dating the Apple Macintosh and Atari ST by two and a half years. One
result of this longevity is that there are of lot of PCs around in the
world, and consequently a lot of music based software. In fact some of
the earliest professional music packages were based on the PC. As the
design of the PC has developed so has the software, becoming not only
more powerful but also cheaper.

One of the great strengths of the PC is its ability to upgrade the
hardware to take advantage of new technologies as they become available, without having to restart from scratch. This feature is also
reflected in a lot of the music software available for the PC, allowing
you to start from modest beginnings and then upgrade as your music
requires a more powerful system.

The Genesis of computers in music

The 1970's saw a virtual revolution in the world of computers
with the introduction by Intel of the first computer on a chip (or microprocessor). With this event we saw the start of the road that took the
computer out of large air-conditioned rooms and into every walk of life.
The introduction of the IBM PC at the beginning of the eighties contin-
ued this trend so that now we are at the stage where we can afford to
have a relatively powerful computer in every home.

The 1980s also saw the application of computers to music in
big way. Whereas in the seventies computer music had been the sole

domain of the rarefied atmosphere of academia, the eighties saw the computer enter into every phase of the production of music from the sound source – in the form of synthesisers – to the production of recorded music – in mixing desk automation and digital sound systems such as the Compact Disc.

The 1990s have ushered in the era of multimedia on personal computers with the introduction of the Multimedia PC (or MPC) specification. This is really an evolutionary step, bringing together the various computing 'threads' that were developed during the previous decade. To the musician, the major benefit of this is the ability to use both MIDI and digital recording techniques on the same platform.

So the computer can be a very useful tool, but it is important to realise both its strengths and limitations when contemplating its use. The most obvious – but perhaps least mentioned – aspect of using a computer in a musical context is that it will not substitute for basic musical skills and/or inspiration. What a computer will do for you is to remove or reduce the tedium of certain tasks such as preparing or printing a score. It will also allow free rein to inspiration without requiring you to become a virtuoso on a particular instrument or perhaps even help you to become a competent performer on that instrument. It may even suggest avenues of composition, but you need to be able to take advantage of the opportunities provided, the 'There Ain't No Such Thing As A Free Lunch' principle still applies.

History of the personal computer in music

In the late seventies, before the IBM PC appeared on the scene, there were a number of small computers which gave people access to computer facilities. These facilities had previously been available only to large corporations and educational institutions that could afford the massive costs involved with mainframe and mini computers. Two popular early microcomputers were the Commodore PET and the Apple II which were both introduced in 1977; the Apple II was very much the trend setter in personal computing incorporating, as it did, eight expansion slots. However, in general the marketplace was fragmented, the equipment was relatively expensive and more importantly there was very little in the way of compatibility between different computers. This meant that peripheral hardware was very costly and rare. Despite this, some musicians saw how useful a computer could be and a few music systems (mainly based on the Apple II) were available. As early as 1977 the respected computer magazine *Byte* had articles about practical music based software and other music-related topics.

When International Business Machines (IBM) introduced its Personal Computer (or PC) in August 1981 it soon became arguably the most successful computer of all time, and the fact that it had the IBM logo on the front ensured that it was taken seriously from the start. The original PC was based on an Intel 8088 microprocessor running at a clock speed of 4.77 megahertz. It came either in a business configuration with 64 kilobytes of RAM, 40 kilobytes of ROM, a monochrome (text only) display and a single 5.25 inch floppy disk, or for home use with 16 kilobytes of RAM with a cassette interface. And at just over $3,000 for the business machine this was equivalent to about $5,000 at today's prices; this would now buy you a quality Pentium PC with a colour Super VGA graphics accelerator, a large VDU and a 500 megabyte hard disk.

One of the most important factors in the popularity of the PC is the fact that it has what's known as an 'open architecture'. This means that IBM made the technical specification of the PC available to other manufacturers so that they could produce expansion cards for it. This policy had an unfortunate side effect as far as IBM was concerned, the makers of the expansion cards had enough information to produce virtually identical copies of the PC. These copies were referred as compatibles (or clones) and were often produced to a superior specification or lower cost (or both!).

So the feature that has ensured the survival of the PC for almost a decade is also the basic design concept behind the PC, expandability. Like the Apple II before it, the IBM PC could be fitted with expansion circuit boards (or cards) to allow it to interface to almost any other device. This adaptability has allowed the PC to keep up with technological advances and for it to be used for purposes of which the designers never dreamed. It is a matter of record that the designers of the PC never expected the proliferation of expansion cards that occurred. This explains why it can be difficult to install multiple cards without having them interfere with each other, an example of the PC being a victim of its own success!

Still, the impact of the personal computer on music production would not be nearly as profound as it has been if it hadn't been for a not entirely unrelated development in the music equipment world. This development was the introduction and ratification of the MIDI specification in 1983. To understand how to use a PC to make music with MIDI, you first need to know a bit about the history of the synthesiser.

The MIDI revolution

In the early 1980's microprocessors were being introduced into the designs of synthesisers. This meant that a computer was being used to detect which keys were being pressed and then used this information to generate sounds. This digitisation of the keyboard 'performance' enabled the keyboard to be separated from the sound modules, the notes to be played being sent down a single cable or serial link. This gave keyboard players the freedom of movement on stage that guitarists enjoyed, since only the keyboard needed to be carried around, connected to the sound modules by this serial cable.

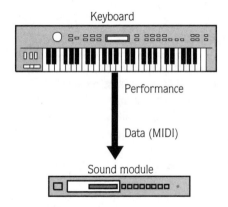

Figure 1.1 Modern synthesisers separate the performance detection from the sound generators

Of course each manufacturer had their own serial interface standard, which meant that you couldn't mix and match keyboards and sound modules made by different companies. Then something wonderful happened. In 1981 a group of manufacturers led by Sequential Circuits, Oberheim and Roland started working on a common standard for the communication of musical performance data. This standard became the Musical Instrument Digital Interface (MIDI), and has been almost universally adopted by the music industry.

How MIDI works

You've probably noticed that we have been stressing the word performance, this is because MIDI doesn't carry the actual sound, rather, it carries the data describing the notes being played. It is up to the synthesiser or sound module to produce the sound. The information is transferred using messages that define each musical event, so a Note On message is sent when you press a key on the keyboard and a Note Off message is sent when you lift your finger off the key. MIDI not only defines which notes are played, it also defines how they can be altered by the performer. Performance parameters that can be sent include volume control, pitch bend and modulation.

However, MIDI is more that just connecting up two synthesisers. Another of the original aims of the MIDI standard was to simplify the interconnection of different synthesiser systems. Therefore, it allows you to control up to 16 instruments independently with synchronisation and control messages – all using a single cable!

Like the PC design, MIDI is now being used for purposes that the original designers never foresaw, this is attributable (in the main) to good design. For instance, one feature of MIDI that makes it 'future proof' is the System Exclusive message. This allows each manufacturer to define their own special message types – called System Exclusive messages – for use with their products. This feature is usually used to allow access to the internal controls of the MIDI device, such as voice programming data or internal set-ups or special features on the synthesiser that are not covered by the MIDI specification.

Whilst the System Exclusive element of the MIDI specification was originally designed to be used solely by instrument manufacturers for configuring their equipment, it has also provided a useful mechanism for expanding the original MIDI specification. Thus the specification has been added to over the years, incorporating new features, mainly relating to the control and interconnection of MIDI instruments. Like the IBM PC design, MIDI is an 'open architecture', it lays down basic ground rules for interconnection without enforcing restrictions which might limit future developments.

What you can do with MIDI

So where does the PC come into this? It's simple really, the MIDI data stream is just a stream of bytes like any other (like the RS232 signal used to connect to printers for instance). The PC can receive the MIDI data, note the time the data was received and then store both these quantities into memory or onto disk. While the data is in memory it can be manipulated like text in a word processor, so it can be displayed, modified and printed in the same way as a document.

At some later date, we can make the computer play back the information to the synthesiser (or another) via MIDI. The synthesiser will then sound the notes as if they were being played by you. It's sort of like an electronic Player Piano except that you don't need scissors and sticky tape to edit the performance. This type of program is called a sequencer, since it preserves the time sequence of the notes and other performance parameters. Sequencers, however, do more than just play back and edit a single performance, they also allow you to manipulate the music in a number of ways. Also, since each MIDI port can control up to 16 channels, you can 'record' up to 16 parts and then play them back together to give an ensemble. This is very handy for composition or song writing, since you can hear or 'demo' your material as you write it.

MIDI control

There is another way that you can use a PC with musical instruments, which is to control their internal circuitry. To explain this we need to go back to the history of the synthesiser again.

If we go back to old analogue synthesisers (like the Mini-Moog), we notice that each parameter of each sound generator (or voice) had a separate knob to control it. However knobs are expensive and a modern synthesiser would require rather a lot of them, so to bring the cost of manufacture down, the knobs have been dispensed with and instead one control is now used to alter each voice parameter. Using buttons to select between the different voice parameters and a small display, you can still change any parameter, but the whole thing has become difficult to visualise as you can't see the voice set-up at a glance.

Again the PC can help out; a lot more information can be displayed on the computer's screen than on the little display on the synthesiser. So, using System Exclusive messages, the PC can edit the internal memory of the synthesiser, altering the sounds and other features, such as effects processors. The information can also be stored on disk, saving to disk is a lot easier than using the cassette interface built into most synthesisers and a lot cheaper than RAM cartridges (that is if your

7

synthesiser can use them). So most brands of synthesiser now have voice (or patch) editors available. These allow you to create your own sounds, load different pre-programmed voices into your synthesiser or even randomly generate sounds.

This also applies to sampling keyboards and other external sound sampling devices; there are programs available that allow you to download a sound sample into the internal memory of the computer, edit it and then send it back. Thus you can 'fine tune' your samples, store them on your computer disk, even do things such as combine different samples to create hybrid sounds.

Other music applications

Scoring

Using a computer to print music is on the surface probably the most obvious and straightforward application outlined in this book. However the potential scope for scoring software is vast, and major differences exist between the many music printing packages available. Simple music printing software can call up the various music symbols for the user to arrange on screen. Other software will take an actual performance from MIDI instruments and score it out automatically. There are the possibilities of part extraction from large scores, transposition, alignment of large scores, reduction of large scores to piano staff, harmonic analysis, full MIDI playback, custom symbol design, integration with page layout programs, and more. In the chapter on scoring many of these features are explored in detail, and more importantly the problems that computers encounter when faced with the task of printing music are brought to light.

Teaching aids

It is a fact that simply using a computer to produce music teaches you many things about music. For instance if you are using your computer to sequence a drum machine, you cannot help learning how a drummer plays, since certain patterns and combinations will sound good whilst others won't. If you are sequencing an orchestral sound module, you cannot fail to notice that in certain music the horns sound great a fifth apart, or that a flute does very little of use below middle C. Orchestration technique is just one of the skills which the computer can help develop.

There is also dedicated music teaching software available designed to develop specific skills. For instance the computer wili play a chord, which has to be recognised by the student, or it will play a pattern of notes which have to be repeated. Scoring software teaches music notation, and sound editing software trains the ear to hear the subtleties of different tones. One thing music software will not teach you though, is anything about computers!

Sound generation on the PC

Although MIDI control of electronic musical instruments is the most common form of producing music with a PC, it's not the only way. Recent developments in Digital Signal Processors (or DSPs) and MPC sound technology have meant that it is possible for manufacturers to produce digital audio expansion cards for the PC. These soundcards can be used to record or replay sounds stored in the PC's internal memory or can be programmed to generate sounds using traditional or experimental digital synthesis methods.

A DSP is essentially a very high speed microprocessor which has been optimised for dealing with analogue signals in real time. DSPs have been around for some time – CD players and digital reverbs are examples of devices that could not exist without DSPs. Though games quality soundcards are now almost 'throw-away' items, to get true 'CD quality' audio from a PC a great deal of care must be exercised in the design of the soundcard, which is usually not compatible with the low cost required by an audio card designed to appeal to the games market. However the cost of high quality cards has been coming down, so, though the relative difference between cards designed for music and those for games use will be maintained, in absolute terms, the cost of CD quality sound on the PC is now well within the ambit of computer musicians.

The use of digital audio as a synthesis tool is perhaps the most powerful method for generating music using your computer, since the sounds or timbres are not limited to those available from commercial instruments. Digital audio soundcards can also form the basis of direct-to-disk recording systems, allowing the PC to replace the tape machine, thus giving all the advantages of digital sound and the added bonus of being able to edit the recording on the computer. With the advent of the Windows tasking operating environment, you can even

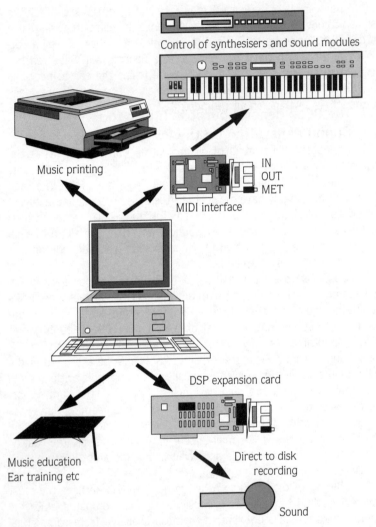

Figure 1.2 Some of the musical possibilities of the PC

run a MIDI sequencer on the same PC as the hard disk recorder, giving you the best of both worlds.

And digital audio soundcards are not the only way for the PC to actually produce the sound. The electronic components used in modern synthesisers are compact enough to be mounted on an internal expansion card for the PC. As the Windows MPC specification incorporates both digital audio and MIDI facilities on a soundcard, you can do away with much of the external paraphernalia to get a powerful but compact computer music workstation. And new technologies like Yamaha's VL (or physical modelling) will take PC based sound generation up to the next level.

The PC, a general purpose music tool

So you can see that the PC can be used in a wide range of musical applications, and if you are inclined to do a bit of programming, these applications are limited only by your imagination. The great strength of any computer – and this includes the PC – is that it is a general purpose tool. Conversely, if you buy a hardware sequencer or sampler, you'll undoubtedly get the same amount of functionality as a computer based system, but you'll be stuck with it from then on. The computer-based system can grow to suit your changing needs and improvements in music technology.

The next chapter will tell you all you need to know about producing high quality scores on the PC. This is followed by a chapter showing how you can interface your computer to MIDI systems. Later chapters cover various software and hardware options available to the computer musician. The final chapter gives an overview of the various types of PC and shows some example systems and how you might use them in different musical environments.

Music as text – scoring

Computers have revolutionised the world of graphics, word processing and publishing. What about musical notation? If a computer can print out a letter, then why can't it print out a musical score? Well, it can, but as we will see, the precise nature of a computer is often a hindrance when involved with musical notation.

If we look at how European music notation has developed we see that by the 7th century graphical symbols – or neumes – were used to represent the approximate time-values and relative pitches of notes. Relics of this system still exist in modern notation as the trill or turn. As time passed the neume system developed more precision, first by adding a staff, which began as a single line, and then by defining the note shapes to indicate definite time-values. Our present day musical notation is therefore based on a graphical representation of the music rather than a direct and precise transcription. It is when things are not defined and 'open to interpretation' that computers have problems!

The results of asking a computer to play back a score from memory and to score a piece played into it are often not what we expect. While not wishing to bore the reader who does not read music, by illustrating the complexity and subtlety of musical notation, it is important to highlight areas for potential problems, so that expectations from scoring software are realistic. If you expect to play your masterpiece into a computer, have the computer print out the equivalent in musical notation, and then for a player to reproduce your piece by reading the print-out directly ... you'll be disappointed. However, software writers continue to address the problems and challenges of notation transcription, and new updated programs keep on appearing on the market.

Notation programs differ from other music software – e.g. a sequencer – in that the end product is designed to be the printed page, rather than a playback performance, or the control of another musical device. The scope for a notation program is enormous; not everyone wants to reprint a simple melody line, and anyone accustomed to modern classical composers' scores will know how strange they can look. In addition to on-screen presentation, the program must tackle the major areas of print format, real-time MIDI input, and the complex editing of music. Obviously there are degrees of complexity, after all not everyone needs to produce a score for a full orchestra on a regular basis, so it is important to have an idea of your real requirements when you start looking for a scoring package.

What's available

Not surprisingly, there are many notation programs now available for the PC, and their features vary enormously. At the simplest level there are a number of music fonts available for use with Microsoft Windows, and using these with a standard graphics design program is one option for producing scores. The simplest dedicated scoring applications can simply be a drawing program with pre-set musical symbols and the ability to draw staves and bar lines. The program will have no musical knowledge to cope with playback, or the aligning and spacing-notes, and therefore will not be able to transpose or do any other actions requiring a musical intelligence. Such programs tend to be low in price, slow to use (since all spacing and alignment must be done by the user), but often give good results when printing.

At the other extreme are scoring programs that will automatically transcribe a piece played in from a MIDI keyboard, display musical notation with all beaming, alignment and spacing proportioned automatically. It will be able to transpose, part extract, perform harmonic analysis, intelligently re-perform the piece looking for graphic phrasing, tempo and dynamic markings. Such software is relatively expensive and requires a commitment from the purchaser with time and patience to get the best from the program. Such 'high end' scoring applications usually require that the user has a deep knowledge of the conventions of producing a professional score, and are really designed to be used by professional copyists to get the best results.

Entering the music

Step-time input

There are a number of ways of getting the music onto the computer, the simplest of which is to enter the music note by note – ofter referred to as 'step-time'. This is the equivalent of typing a letter on a word processor with all characters entered individually by the user. Looking at available music programs, they offer one or more of the following four methods of step-input.

1   Using a mouse and palette or keystroke codes.
2   From a musical keyboard via MIDI.
3   Using the computer keyboard and a table of codes.
4   By importing a file from other software.

Mouse and palette

Probably the simplest method of input is using a mouse, and certainly programs written for Windows make full use of this option. Typically the software displays a series of palettes containing notes, symbols and markings, and these can be 'clicked' and dragged into position on the stave. The program will to some extent be musically intelligent about the placement of items. For example in programs like Passport's Encore and MusicTime, placing eight individual quavers into the first bar of the stave will give you the following (Figure 2.1):

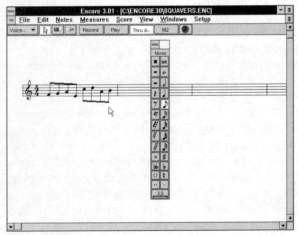

Figure 2.1 Example of automatic format

The program automatically groups and beams the quavers and sorts out spacing, stem length and stem direction. Further note placement within the bar is disallowed due to the time signature, unless the addition is to an existing quaver thus making a chord. Such intelligent assistance from the program is essential if step-entry is to be a viable method of input. The time required to manually beam and position notes (note that in our example the stem length is different for each note) would otherwise be immense.

MIDI keyboard

Other programs use a combination of mouse and keystroke codes for entry. Musicator for Windows still uses the mouse to position notes, but their duration is selected by pressing numbers on the computer keyboard, rather than using a palette. Similarly any accidentals (sharps, flats, etc.) are selected by holding down various keys while clicking the note into position.

Using a MIDI keyboard can further speed up step-time entry. Rather than positioning the note carefully on the stave, the computer receives the pitch information from an attached MIDI device. In our earlier example the notes are all the same duration (quavers) so step-time MIDI input would simply involve selecting the quaver duration and playing the eight notes on the MIDI keyboard. There is no metronome to play to, the computer is not interested in the speed or timing accuracy of our playing –- it just takes the pitch information. This method of entry can be the best and quickest for 'un-skilled' players.

Computer keyboard

The third option for input uses the computer keyboard and a table of text codes, and is mainly favoured by DOS music programs. The DOS version of Note Processor from Thought Processes uses a text line input based on a system called DARMS. DARMS is the acronym for Digital Alternative Representation of Musical Scores, and was initially designed by Stefan Bauer-Mengelberg in 1963.

Figure 2.2 Note processor example

The DARMS input line for the example in Figure 2.2 would be:

!l2 !F !MC !& !U 11RE 11E(E 12) 13 (11 13 14) /
15Q 13 14 11E(12) / 13 /*
& !D 1RE 9E(E 10) 13(11 13 14) /
15(6 9 8) 7Q 6E(5) / \E,4H /* $&

Not surprisingly the program has other methods of input to avoid typing in all that text, but the option is there.

SCORE by Leland Smith (San Andreas Press) is one of the few programs used extensively for professional music typesetting. Its design was based on requirements for that specific industry, that is, how to get a page of music from handwritten manuscript to high quality print in the shortest time. Interestingly it uses a similar text input system. On the input line, C4 is used as the code for middle C, C5 for the octave above etc., a slash separates notes, and a colon indicates notes that belong to the same chord.

So the input line for a C major triad followed by a D and E would be:

C4:E4:G4/D4/E4

SCORE goes on to use this method for the input of rhythms, markings, etc., all of which use a separate line of text for entry. After entering the pitches and rhythms, the program will correctly space the notes on the stave according to their value, or align them with another stave in the system.

Figure 2.3 SCORE example

This type of text input allows integration with other software, as the input file can usually be saved and re-imported as a text file.

MIDISCORWRITE from New Notations is a program specifically written to convert Standard MIDI Files produced by a sequencer program into SCORE text files. Similarly the text files produced by SCORE can be converted into a MIDI File (MIDISCORE – New Notations).

While the text line is fundamental to SCORE's input system, the program also allows MIDI input to create the text. Pressing middle C on the MIDI keyboard will write C4 into the text input line shown on screen. The program also uses an assignable octave on the input MIDI keyboard, usually the bottom octave, to input other items of text relating to the codes for rhythmic values, accidentals, etc. So despite being a text input based program, most of music entry is possible without leaving the musical keyboard.

File import

The fourth method of input discussed in this section is the import of a file. The most relevant file to import is a Standard MIDI File – a file of 'performance' music created by a sequencer, and recognised by its .MID extension (sometimes .SMF). MIDI files can be bought from specialist companies, found on bulletin boards, and are created by most computer sequencers. Their format is identical regardless of which computer and program originally created the file (although the physical disk format may vary between different computers).

Because MIDI files contain real-time information, the next section, which highlights the way music programs handle musical timing, is also relevant to any discussion on importing MIDI files.

The way music software handles pitch information is also relevant here, as different programs interpret MIDI files in different ways. SCORE has programmed defaults that assume that the chromatic notes on the 3rd and 7th of the major scale will be flats (or naturals in a sharp key), and that the chromatic 2nd, 4th and 5th notes will be sharps. So playing the black notes in the key of C will result in Figure 2.4.

Figure 2.4 Accidental defaults – SCORE

A simple example illustrating pitch interpretation, is to create a MIDI file (in a sequencer program) containing one bar of 4 crotchets – C#, D#, F# and G#. Importing this file into Personal Composer and Musicator for Windows gives Figure 2.5. Importing the file into Encore

Figure 2.5 MIDI file transcription example – imported into Personal Composer and Musicator for Windows

and MusicTime gives the same accidentals as our SCORE example in Fig 2.4, while Finale notates the file differently again; Figure 2.6.

Figure 2.6 Second MIDI file transcription example – imported into Finale

The same file has been interpreted and displayed in three different ways. Once imported, all programs will let you set the key signature for the piece. In our example changing the key signature to C# minor gives Figure 2.7, except for Musicator which gives the result Figure 2.8

Figure 2.7 MIDI file transcription after key change to C# minor

Figure 2.8 MIDI file transcription after key change to C# minor in Musicator

The reader may possibly regard the discussion as trivial; but it is precisely these types of features and discrepancies between programs that will determine how much editing the user will have to do before final print out. The program may prompt you, as do Finale and Personal Composer, to set details about the file you are about to import, such as key signature, quantisation, which can result in a closer first attempt at notating the file. Finale has the interesting added option of guessing the key signature of the file it's about to import. (In our example above it guessed Db major as the key.)

As we move on to look at real-time input in the next section, programs still have the task of interpreting keys and accidentals, but in addition there's the immediate timing of the input data to resolve.

Real-time input

The real-time entry of music is through MIDI from a keyboard or other MIDI device. The question of whether to include a real-time MIDI input or a step-time implementation, must give program designers plenty to consider. For those who are unsure of the terms step-time and real-time; real-time implies that the player plays – usually in-time with a metronome generated by the computer – and the program analyses and transcribes the duration values of the notes (the rhythm) as well as the pitches; step-time implies that the program analyses only the pitches of notes. The argument against real-time input, is that it takes longer to edit out performance mistakes and misunderstandings of rhythm, than it would do to enter the duration values for notes manually from the computer keyboard. The argument for real-time input is that it's the most ideal use of a computer for music; the computer records a performance and prints out the score!

The real-time MIDI input presents interesting problems for software programs, mainly because compared to computer accuracy, very few players can play in time. Consider the simple task of playing one crotchet per beat. The player may be able to get the beginning of the note in time with the metronome, but note endings, when you lift your finger up to play the next note, are often very scrappy. Obviously a computer will pick up on this and interpret a shortened note as a dotted quaver followed by a rest or similar. If we hold a note on slightly too long, but play the next note on time on the beat, the computer will interpret that as a momentary chord on that beat. Then the computer has to decide whether this seemingly simple piece is in two parts, stems up and stems down.

This potential confusion is from simple crotchets on the beat, imagine a complex two handed piano improvisation. To take the example to the extreme – at a tempo of 120bpm the crotchets should last exactly 0.5 seconds; any longer or any shorter and the computer is quite justified in notating them differently. Therefore the performance you play for a computer to notate must be extremely strict in tempo and pitch, and must be played with the consideration that the music you want to se, is not necessarily the music you want to hear. It is the performer that puts life into the score in front of him on a piece of paper, by taking into account phrasing marks, pedalling, legato, rubato.

One of the major difficulties of real-time input is that the computer usually dictates the tempo, and will not change or flex unless pre-programmed to do so. The result is that the natural slowing down at the end of each phrase, or the continual give and take (rubato) within a performance, will be interpreted by the computer as you playing out of time, and thus it will faithfully reproduce your notes either in the next or previous bar, or off the beat! The result is a score that is unreadable to a player, nothing like you expected, and which requires extensive editing to make presentable.

Obviously the simpler the music the more likely the computer is to get it right, or rather the more likely the player is to play it right. Similarly, the more understanding the player is to the computer's 'way of thinking' the better the results. Editing facilities within programs that accept real-time information are therefore very important and are discussed in more detail later in the chapter.

Consider our simple scale of C major over two bars in crotchets on the beat. The score we are looking for is this: (Figure 2.9)

Figure 2.9 C major scale; two bars in crotchets

The score we may get due to our inaccuracies in playing may be this (Figure 2.10):

Figure 2.10 Possible notation of our performance of Figure 2.9

If the program allows only graphic editing (i.e. the cut, copy and paste of single graphic symbols) we are left with a major editing task, with nearly every note having to be repositioned, such that our real-time performance was a waste of time.

By applying quantising to our real-time input, the computer can make the best use of our poor performance. Quantising shifts the notes onto the nearest beat or division of a beat, so that if in our example above we quantised to quarter notes (or crotchets), the result would be closer to what we wanted, as the start of each note would shift to the nearest crotchet beat. Further quantisation of note durations to crotchets, would achieve the correct notation. However if bar three (not shown) contained quavers, these would also be quantised to crotchets and we would lose the required transcription of bar three. If we had quantised the whole piece to quavers (eighth notes), we would have probably been all right for bars one, two and three, but if bar four has triplets in it, we're in trouble again. In this case it can often be an advantage to use a sequencer to record the performance and to prepare it for import into a notation program as a MIDI file.

Notation versus sequencing

A sequencer program usually offers a more flexible and complex editing system where rhythms and note durations can be tidied up. For instance in Voyetra's Sequencer Plus series, different sections can be quantised to different resolutions, for example, the one bar of demi-semiquavers can be quantised as such while the rest of the section can be quantised in quavers (8s). There's also the option to quantise both start-times and note durations. Editing the file in this way offers a better chance of the scoring program correctly notating the piece. Here, you may end up with two versions of your composition, one that sounds great when performed by the sequencer, and one that sounds very boring but transcribes well when imported by a scoring program. The sequencer provides an opportunity to edit a performance before the computer attempts to transcribe it into musical notation.

The example simply shows that quantising can do much to iron out imperfections in performance picked up in the computer's transcription, but it can also restrict other areas in the performance that require a finer or different quantisation.

Finale from Coda Music tackles the problem of real-time input in a unique way. It allows the player to give a tempo indication to the computer during the performance of the piece, so there is no need to play to a strict metronome. Any variations in tempo during performance can be played without the computer getting out of step and misinterpreting the notation. The player first tells the program which MIDI event will dictate the tempo; this may be a particular note, or a foot switch, or any other MIDI data. Then the rate of the event is set, i.e. if you are tapping your foot on a foot switch, whether you are tapping in crotchets, minims, quavers, etc. The software is set into record, and as soon as it receives the first MIDI tempo event, beat one of bar one is set and the recording begins. Only on receiving the next tempo indicator (beat two) will the computer know how to notate the notes played between the two beats.

Some of the more advanced programs successfully bridge the gap between notation and sequencing by being pretty good at both. The MIDI performance is held in memory and can be edited in various ways (see Chapter 4 on sequencing); it can also be viewed as notation, and, depending on its appearance, can be edited directly, or the performance file modified and then re-notated before printing. The only problem with this approach is that the score displayed on the screen is not the same as the original performance that is stored in the computer's memory, which can cause a certain amount of confusion during the editing process.

Printing output

The quality of the printed output is obviously one of the most important features of any notation program. With DOS-based notation software especially, the output quality can vary enormously between different programs. Usually the software writer has had the job of drawing the individual musical symbols, and the quality of these is worth investigating on sample printouts. Again with DOS based software, it is especially important to check whether the software supports your particular printer, and whether the option for A4 paper size exists alongside the ever dominant US letter size.

Windows notation software has the advantage of being able to print to any Windows installed printer. The program will include the appropriate music fonts sometimes giving a choice between True Type and Postscript fonts. For lyrics, titles, copyright notices and other text based markings, the program should allow choice from any of the installed Windows fonts. (With DOS based programs you will often be limited to those fonts included with the software.) If you're thinking of buying a program, either DOS based, or for Windows, it is well worth viewing print-outs, preferably on the printer you intend to use.

Printing options relating to the overall format of the score are worth considering. For instance offsets and size reductions are useful if you intend to make a book directly from your printouts. Also a landscape format is useful for some scores (e.g. Organ Music).

Larger orchestral scores require special consideration, and programs usually limit the possible size of a score by restricting the number of systems per page and the number of staves per system. (A vocal score for soprano, alto, tenor and bass has four staves per system.) For example Cakewalk 3 for Windows sets limits of 24 staves per page, Encore and Cubase Score 64 staves and Finale 128; Personal Composer has limits of 42 staves per system and 12 systems per page.

Such large scores may run into more problems when printing since most software prints only to A4 paper. One way to overcome this is to print to file (EPS – Encapsulated Postscript format) and use a specialised bureau for printing, or a cheaper method is assembling pages manually after print out and photocopying them onto larger paper! (so much for automation!).

Playback of scores

The playback facilities for scores vary tremendously between different programs. At worst there will be no means of playback at all. This tends to be from programs that have little or no musical intelligence and are working as simple graphics or drawing software. Next come the programs that use the PC speaker for playback, such as Songwright 5 and SCORE (note that these programs also have MIDI playback facilities). The only real advantage of such playback is that it does not require the additional expense of a soundcard or MIDI adapter. The limitations are considerable; firstly the only tone available is the familiar beep you get when you turn on your PC; the beep can be lengthened to create different note values and changed in pitch to give melody lines, it cannot however be polyphonic, and so is limited to playing only single note melody lines. Chords cannot be played and the option is sometimes given either to arpeggiate the chord or just play the top note. To summarise, playback from the PC speaker is of little use for polyphonic pieces, but can be sufficient for music tuition software, or simple melody-line printing programs.

The playback of scores using MIDI or a soundcard has the advantage of offering full polyphony and the possibility of correctly assigning instruments to their appropriate parts in the score. This obviously assumes that you have the MIDI equipment or soundcard that can cope with the polyphony and multitimbral requirements of the score. Scoring programs that are also sequencers, such as Finale, Cubase Score, Cakewalk and Personal Composer have extensive MIDI playback facilities. Cakewalk includes a 256-track sequencer that talks directly to the scoring side of the program. In general terms, staves are assigned to MIDI channels, which allows a particular instrument, chosen by a program change message, to play the notes from that stave.

Windows MPC compatible soundcards and some MIDI equipment feature GM (General MIDI) compatibility, which ensures that program change numbers sent by software call up the same instrument regardless of the soundcard or attached MIDI device (e.g. program change #1 will call up a Grand Piano sound while #49 = strings etc.). This being the case, some programs designed specifically for GM devices, will allow you to call up the instruments for each stave by name.

SCORE offers a limited MIDI playback facility implemented only as an aural proof for a page of music, and in no way attempts to compete with a sequencer in terms of MIDI playback. The program holds only one page in memory at any one time, and consequently can only play back that page, and only four staves at once.

Depending on the program, playback will either be direct from the score as displayed on the screen, or from the sequencer file held in memory from real-time input, or the import of a MIDI file. As discussed, direct score playback will be particularly stilted and lifeless with unnaturally perfect timing and lack of dynamics

Some notation programs, e.g. MusicPrinter Plus, Encore and Finale, will allow the assignment of MIDI values to some score markings that will then be interpreted on playback. Thus staccato dots over notes play back as shortened MIDI notes, a crescendo hair-pin under the stave gives a gradual increase in the loudness of the track; this is achieved by sending notes with an increasing 'velocity' value; – data corresponding to how hard you hit a note on a keyboard. Similarly the MIDI interpretations of tenutos, accents, dynamic markings and tempo indications, can be incorporated into the MIDI performance.

Even when this is possible, the reader should realise that sequencer and notation programs are designed and structured to achieve different results; one a performance, the other a printed page. Trying to get a perfect sounding performance from notation software by editing markings, etc., is hard going in comparison to using a sequencer.

If there is no direct MIDI playback from the score, it is also unlikely that the program will save work as a sequencer file or MIDI file. In general, scoring programs are more likely to import sequencer files than to export them.

Editing scores

The editing capabilities of the scoring program usually depend on the amount of musical intelligence retained after the input stage. Simple graphics or drawing software will allow typical cut, copy and paste operations, often using a mouse or cursor keys to define areas for editing. Software that retains knowledge of note values will be able to reformat pages if notes are added, deleted or moved.

The advantage of a graphic music editing system is that layout is very flexible. Symbols can be placed anywhere, without the program 'snapping' them to positions governed by its pre-programmed musical rules. Consider the layout of a piece of modern music, with graphic symbols combined with some notes, shapes, lines, etc., text often in mid-stave; or medieval music with a four line stave and no time signature; or, more commonly, a split note beam between bass and treble clefs. Such music often causes problems to programs that apply a musical intelligence to the layout by controlling the spacing and alignment of notes. When automatic features cannot be manually over-ridden, some scores simply cannot be completed using that program.

Programs such as Songwright 5 allow the user to step through each item-note, rest, etc., and display the attributes of the current item; for example 'C-4, crotchet, stem-up'. Changes are made by editing the text attributes associated with that item, and on confirmation, the graphic will change on screen, and the bar will re-format if necessary. SCORE uses the same idea of parameters for each item, but takes it much further. When selecting an item for editing, the program displays a table of up to 18 numbers each governing different attributes. For example for a note there are parameters governing size, position, rhythmic value, stem length, type of note head, the staff it is 'attached' to, and markings on the note. For a slur there are parameters governing start and end points, vertical positions, thickness of slur, curvature, etc.; changing any parameter will modify the graphic on screen, and the program will then re-format and re-justify the edited line of music.

SCORE has probably the most comprehensive editing system of all the notation programs. Powerful editing controls include the alignment of notes on multi-stave systems. Consider a large orchestral score of 32 staves, SCORE will align all notes together vertically, taking into account the spacing of notes, markings, graphics, and lyrics on each stave. The condition of course is that each bar of each stave has the same number of beats; if not, SCORE will let you know that it cannot justify the page as it stands. Any mistakes or further alterations to that page can be corrected by selecting items and changing the appropriate parameters. If this results in a different positioning of the note (for instance adding an accidental to a note will often require it to be displaced to make room), then the whole score can be re-aligned automatically. SCORE allows all of its automatic features to be overridden, and can therefore be used as a simple music graphics program with a large library of symbols.

Retaining a musical intelligence ensures that programs have no problem in transposing music, extracting parts from scores, re-sizing staves within systems (for cue parts, etc.) and retaining alignment.

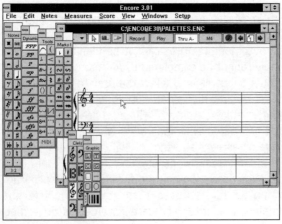

Figure 2.11 Editing with palettes – Encore

In the Windows environment, editing usually involves using a series of palettes (i.e. 'floating' toolbars) that hold the symbols for notes, rests, markings, text, etc. (Figure 2.11). Dynamic markings such as accents and staccato dots become 'attached' to the notes so that they move with the note when music is reformatted, transposed, or parts are extracted. Typically common editing features are transposition, change of clefs, applications of slurs and ties, expression and dynamic markings and common musical symbols.

Advanced features

It is worth seriously considering the complexity of the scores you wish to notate before choosing your notation program. You may require your software to notate percussion note heads, guitar chords, guitar or lute tablature, harp pedal markings, string bowing marks, ancient music symbols, mini notes, piano pedal symbols, special unique markings for modern scores, accordion buttons – the list is endless; music notation is a complex and vast language.

Most programs allow the input of text freely within a score, either as lyrics or free text, headings, instructions, etc., however if lyrics are fundamental to your requirements for music printing, then look closely at the program's capabilities. Programs that automatically control the spacing and alignment of notes, may give problems when trying to fit words and syllables underneath individual notes. If notes are too cramped for the accompanying lyrics, you may be stuck unless the spacing can be manually overridden.

However most programs that specifically cater for lyrics have the important facility of being able to justify music according to the text underneath. In SCORE, for example, lyrics are entered as the syllables for each note. The program can then calculate the best spacing considering both the rhythmic value of that note and the physical size of the text associated with it. If the vocal line is then extracted as a part, the text will go with it and be re-formatted accordingly.

Incorporation of music into other computer graphics software is often important. For example in preparing books, exam papers, hymnals, etc., the music content may form a small part of the final page. Often the completion of a page may require the specific features of word processor or page layout program; features not included in a notation program. It may be important therefore that the program can save files in a format accepted by other software. Windows programs and SCORE will allow files or selected areas to be saved as EPS files compatible with many page layout programs. In addition Musicator for Windows allows a selected area to be copied to the clipboard in either bit map (useful for applications such as paintbrush) or vector format (Pagemaker, Word, etc.). Many other programs will not produce compatible files, and traditional paste-up techniques must be used to prepare final artwork.

Before concluding this chapter it is worth mentioning a few advanced features available in some programs, as they often point to future developments in notation software. Finale for example will perform piano reductions of larger scores, and explode piano pieces into four parts. SCORE will automatically transcribe between guitar and lute tablature and standard notation. Programs are now appearing that can scan music from the printed page and convert it into a MIDI file for playback. Then there's the automatic generation of multiple bars rest when producing individual parts from a score. (This ensures that the percussion players don't get 10 pages of music all containing rests!). There's the control over the individual size of each item, be it the length of a note stem to the thickness and curvature of a slur. Programs like Finale and SCORE even give you an integrated drawing program so that you can design your own symbols and note heads.

Hopefully this chapter has introduced you to the vast potential of notation software and to the difficulties that programs have in interpreting what we play. If you're planning on buying some software, then think carefully about the features you require.

Purchase checklist

1 With such a vast choice of scoring programs, all with different features, it is vital that the purchaser puts priority on different aspects. The major questions are:

- Do you really want notation software for printing? Maybe a sequencer program that has a basic notation display will be adequate for your needs.
- Is MIDI input / output important?
- How much real-time sequencing power do you need in the program?
- Are special symbols or non-standard musical notation required?
- Are the scores large and do they require special printing and sizing options?

Use the answers to these questions to determine the type and the price range of potential programs.

2 Check the computer requirements for the software; memory, video standard, mouse, computer speed, options for maths co-processor. Also check whether the software requires Windows.

3 If MIDI input or output is specified, check which MIDI interface or soundcard is supported. This qualification only really applies with DOS based applications since Windows 3.1 and Windows 95 will allow any MPC supported soundcard to be used, though you may like to consider the quality of the soundcard's audio output.

4 Check the program's printer options. Is your printer supported; can a file be taken to other higher quality printers if necessary? Again this is only really an issue with DOS based applications since Windows programs should work with any graphic printer that has a Windows driver.

5 Does the program output files which can be read by other software, and will the program import files from other programs (e.g. sequencer files)? Are standard MIDI files supported for either input and/or output?

6 Is there an upgrade path to more comprehensive products should the software not meet the requirements for future scoring work?

7 Are the editing, layout and automatic features that you require included?

The MIDI connection

If you want to make music rather than produce a musical score, one of the simplest ways to produce high quality sound with the PC is to use it to control a music synthesiser. This lets you use the computing power of the PC whilst getting the high quality sounds that can be produced on commercially available synthesisers. That this is possible is almost solely due to the development of the MIDI standard as detailed in Chapter 1.

This method of making music is attractive for a number of reasons, the major one being that there is a whole wealth of different sound generation technologies available at quite a reasonable price. It also makes sense to use a dedicated sound synthesiser as the amount of work that the computer is required to perform to produce reasonable sound quality prevents it from doing anything much else. Of course the synthesiser doesn't have to be external to the PC, there are a growing number of PC expansion card based synthesisers becoming available, both dedicated music cards or as part of a Windows MPC soundcard.

The disadvantage of this approach is that the types of sound that can be produced are limited to what is available in commercial synthesisers (or soundcards). This means that totally new sounds can't be generated, only patched together using the sound modules. This however is not going be much of a limitation if your main intent is to make music – rather than design new sounds. There is a wide range of different types of sound available using modern synthesisers, from totally electronically generated sounds to electronically regenerated acoustic

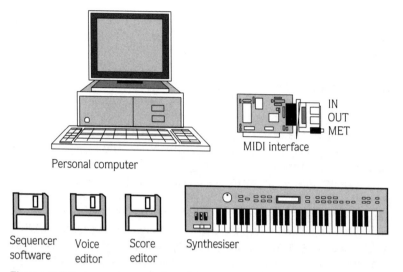

IN
OUT
MET

MIDI interface

Personal computer

Sequencer software   Voice editor   Score editor   Synthesiser

Figure 3.1 Basic requirements for a PC-based MIDI system

instrument sounds. It is also possible to generate entirely new sounds from the PC with the addition of appropriate hardware, this subject is covered in Chapter 6.

What is MIDI?

As mentioned in Chapter 1, the MIDI protocol is essentially a high speed serial link. Unfortunately however, the bit (or baud) rate of MIDI is not one to which a standard PC serial port can be configured. For the PC to handle MIDI information a special piece of hardware – called a MIDI interface – must be fitted to the computer. This interface can either be fitted into one of the internal expansion slots inside the PC or attached externally to one of the serial or parallel (i.e. printer) ports.

The MIDI protocol, as it was developed between 1981 and 1983, was a compromise between performance response and processor speed. At the time most synthesisers were based on eight bit micro-processors with a clock speed of 2MHz. The designers set the speed of the MIDI data transfer at the upper limit of what was technically feasible at the time. Indeed some early MIDI synthesisers had a habit of leaving notes sounding if too much MIDI information was sent to them. This effect was caused by the microprocessor in the synthe-siser not being able to keep up with the incoming MIDI transmission and missing or losing some of the MIDI data.

Actually, the issue of the speed of transmission of the MIDI data is a bit of a red herring, since it is not necessarily the overall data transfer rate that is the most important factor during a 'live' perfor-mance. What is important is that there should be as small a delay as possible between a note being pressed on the keyboard and the infor-mation being read (and acted on) by the MIDI synthesiser. This time delay is usually referred to as the note 'latency' of the system.

Under normal performance situations, the amount of data being sent via MIDI is quite small, this is referred to as the data 'throughput'. The relatively high data rate of the MIDI link is designed to reduce the latency to a point were the musician – and the audience – won't notice it. This is fine in a performance situation, where you might only have one or two instruments using a MIDI cable, but things get a bit more complicated when MIDI is used for sequencing, as you may have up to 16 instruments involved.

So the parties to the original MIDI agreement set the MIDI data rate to 31.25 kilobaud (or 31,250 bits per second) which was about as fast as the microprocessors available at the end of 1983 could reli-ably handle. In case you are wondering why that number was chosen, it just happens to be an even multiple of the 2MHz processor clock speed of the systems of the time.

This data rate can be translated into a delay, since a MIDI note message consists of three MIDI 'bytes', and a MIDI 'byte' is actually ten 'bits'. This gives us a delay of just under a millisecond between the key being pressed and the synthesiser detecting the note message; this delay is imperceptible, which is the entire point of the high speed of MIDI transmission.

However if you have a lot of notes all playing at the same time then things get more complicated. If you consider a General MIDI (or GM) sound module with the ability to play 24 notes simultaneously, then – since the MIDI cable can carry only one note at a time – you could get up to a 20 millisecond delay which is probably perceptible to most musicians. Fortunately this doesn't happen very often, but the potential is there for a perceptible delay.

Why a separate interface is necessary

Some personal computers, such as the Apple Macintosh or the Commodore Amiga, can be interfaced to MIDI by the addition of a simple voltage to current converter to one of their serial ports. Indeed the Atari ST has this converter already built in. Unfortunately, this simple solution is not possible on the PC. When the PC was introduced in 1981, serial interfaces tended to be much less sophisticated than they are today, since they operated at relatively low data rates. As the interfaces on the PC and the various 'clones' have to be compatible, the PC interface specification has never been upgraded. It is a common misconception that the PC serial interface is not 'fast' enough to handle the MIDI data rate. This is not the case. The problem with the PC's serial port is that it can't be set to the correct MIDI data rate. It can go faster or slower, but it can't be set to exactly 31.25 kilobaud.

This is somewhat of a problem when using the PC for MIDI applications, since you need to purchase a dedicated MIDI interface. Other personal computers that came onto the scene later, such as the Apple Macintosh and the Commodore Amiga have more versatile serial ports which can handle the MIDI data rate. So all they need is a buffer box to convert the RS232 levels into the 5mA current loop signal used by MIDI.

The original MIDI cards available for the PC did tend to be more reliable than the simple interfaces found on other personal computers since they incorporated a certain amount of intelligence. These intelligent interfaces – almost always based on the Roland MPU-401 'standard' – could produce more powerful and reliable MIDI systems by offloading some of the processing chores from the computer's main processor. This had the effect of reducing the note latency, which is the most important part of handling MIDI data as far as the musician is concerned. Other advantages include the addition of extra facilities such as a metronome output and synchronisation. Recently, serial port MIDI interfaces have become more commonly available for the PC but they need to be more sophisticated – and thus more expensive – than their Macintosh or Amiga equivalents since they must convert between two different serial data rates.

With the introduction of more powerful PCs the need for intelligent MIDI interfaces declined since the processors had enough spare capacity to handle the load imposed by handling the MIDI data stream. Also, enhancements of the MIDI specification to include features like

MIDI timecode (i.e. MTC) meant that the intelligent features of existing cards based on the Roland chip-set could no longer be used, since there was no way of updating the in-built firmware that resided on the interfaces. Consequently 'intelligent' MIDI cards have more or less fallen out of use except for some specialised DOS applications and some DOS based computer games.

The advent of Windows 3.1 caused the biggest shake-up of the PC MIDI interface market since the introduction of the PC as it removed the requirement that MIDI software authors had to support individual types of MIDI interface. Windows has MIDI support built into the operating environment's Application Programming Interface (or API). This enables software authors to concentrate on processing the MIDI data while letting the interface manufacturer to sort out the 'nuts and bolts' of transferring the MIDI data between their hardware and Windows. Finally, the definition of the Windows Multimedia PC (MPC) standard (which incorporates both an internal synthesiser and the option of an external MIDI interface) has also meant that a plethora of MIDI-equipped soundcards have appeared on the market.

Synchronisation

One of the most interesting musical applications using MIDI is what's called 'sequencing'. This is where a piece of music is stored on the computer and replayed, rather like a multi-track tape recorder. This subject is covered in more detail in Chapter 4, but it is useful at this point to consider the basic elements that make a MIDI sequence since it will help you to choose the best type of interface for your particular musical application.

To faithfully reproduce either a composition or a live performance on a computer you need to do two things. The first is to reproduce the correct pitch, this is very obvious and easily done by storing the MIDI note values. The second element is to preserve the time relationship of the notes, this is somewhat more difficult since not only do we need to store the time with each note, but we need to do this accurately. Research has shown that the human ear can differentiate time intervals down to about five milliseconds, depending on the type of sound. So to have a useful sequencer we need to be able get a timing resolution better than five milliseconds.

Another aspect of sequencing is that it is often necessary for the computer to play in time to other devices. This is because some elements of the music might reside on another instrument, such as a drum machine or even a tape machine. This ability is very important since a lot of music involves vocals of one sort or another. There are also instruments that cannot easily be synthesised; perhaps (for instance), you would like to have that Andean Nose Flute sound for one of your compositions, in which case you would need to record this on tape. This technique is called synchronisation and there are several methods available that allow you to do this. These techniques are described in more detail in Chapter 5, but briefly (in order of sophistication), they are drum click, frequency shift keying (FSK), smart FSK and timecode (SMPTE/EBU and MTC).

Types of interface

MIDI interfaces for the PC fall into three basic categories; internal, external and MPC soundcard based. These vary both in complexity and hardware configuration, and range from simple single-port MIDI devices up to sophisticated multi-port systems with built-in timecode and video facilities. The important thing to remember when you look at adding MIDI to your PC is that by itself, a MIDI interface is useless: it needs to be supported by your software. If you are looking at DOS based systems you must consider what software is available for it (since these programs must be written to support specific interfaces).

For Windows you don't need to worry about each individual MIDI application, but you still need to check that there is a Windows device driver available for the interface. The MIDI device driver is essentially a small program that tells Windows how to communicate with the MIDI interface hardware. The device driver would normally be supplied by the manufacturer of the interface, though there are some third party device drivers available for common interface types. All current MIDI interfaces designed for use with the PC should have a Windows driver. It is also a good idea to check that your chosen interface's device driver is 'multi-client' since this will allow more than one application to use the interface simultaneously.

On the programming side, if you want to create your own MS-DOS based MIDI applications, you must consider whether technical information describing the software interface is available. If you want to write commercial MIDI applications, then you must also consider what interface is most popular, so that you have some potential customers! This last problem has been more or less removed with the advent of Windows since your software will be interfacing with the operating system rather than the actual MIDI hardware.

Simple interfaces

The simplest type of interface that can be fitted to a PC is essentially a standard serial interface card that has been modified to handle the MIDI data rate and signal levels. This type of interface is no longer commercially available, but it is quite simple to build one if you are that way inclined. A complete design for such an interface was published in the June 1986 issue of BYTE magazine.

There is very little software available for this kind of interface so it is really only practicable if you are thinking of writing your own programs. The simple interface is an ideal option if you want a 'home brew' MIDI system that you can easily tinker with, since it is technically quite simple to use. However if you want to have access to the wide range of music software currently available then you need something more sophisticated. This kind of interface has no synchronisation facilities 'built-in' above and beyond what is already present in MIDI. This means that to synchronise to an external device, you'll need to buy some extra equipment.

Intelligent interfaces

The simple interface relies totally on the computer to handle the incoming MIDI data, determine the time relationship of the musical information and then store the data into the PC's internal memory. Whilst the computer is doing this, it cannot do anything else, such as access a disk drive or update the screen, as it may potentially lose data. Even using a multitasking operating environment such as Windows you run the risk of losing data when using a simple interface.

This data loss was a real problem for the early PCs as they were relatively slow, in terms of CPU clock speed. To overcome this problem, Roland developed the first of the Intelligent MIDI interfaces – the MPU-401.

The main difference between the simple interface described in the previous section and the MPU-401 is that the latter has a microprocessor built into it. This extra processor turns the interface into what is essentially another small computer complete with its own software, which is stored in read only memory (ROM) on the card. This software is designed to send and receive MIDI data without needing to interrupt the PC's main processor (or CPU). This, in effect, de-couples the main processor from the nitty gritty of handling the MIDI data as it arrives or departs. The interface can record not only the note as it is received, but also its time relationship in terms of its own accurate internal timebase. This means that the CPU can retrieve the note and the time information at its leisure, allowing it to do such things as update the video display, read the keyboard and hard disk drive without being interrupted.

Apart from the handling of the MIDI note data, the intelligent interface can also perform other related tasks. For instance the original Roland card had the basic facilities for synchronising the computer to various external devices and also produced an audible metronome to indicate the chosen tempo to the musician. The synchronisation facilities allowed you to either 'slave' other devices such as drum machines to the computer, or alternatively to get the PC to play in time with either a tape machine or some other musical device. Unfortunately the Roland MPU-401 was designed before MTC (MIDI timecode) was added to the MIDI specification, which means that there is no way of synchronising its internal timebase to this protocol.

This extra processor has an additional effect on the PC music system, the note latency is reduced. This latency is the time between when a note actually occurred and when it was detected by the computer. Obviously this timing error should be as small as possible for accurate representation of the musical performance. The processor on an intelligent interface is dedicated to handling MIDI data, so it can be optimised for receiving MIDI whereas the PC's main processor has a number of other important tasks that it must perform whilst it is running your music software. Incidentally, the lack of MTC facilities is not fatal to the use of this type of card, it just means that the software can't use some of the advanced features available, in effect using the card as if it were a simple interface.

The MPU-401 family of MIDI interfaces

The MPU-401 has become a very popular interface because of these intelligent features and also due to the fact that Roland made the details of the software and hardware interface completely public. They also sold the custom integrated circuits (or ICs) to any other manufacturers who wished to make compatible MIDI cards. This piece of far-sighted policy has made the Roland specification almost universal amongst DOS music software for the PC. And, if a number of different interfaces are supported by a piece of software, one of them will almost certainly be the MPU-401.

Roland no longer makes the original MPU-401, there is now a more compact version called the MPU-401-AT. However Roland still sell the MPU chipset to other manufacturers such as Voyetra who produce an add-on daughter board to add an MPU-401 compatibility to their V22 and V24 interfaces. There are also a few smaller specialist manufacturers in the professional audio visual world who produce Roland compatible expansion cards using the Roland chipset.

All 100% MPU compatible interfaces have one MIDI input and one MIDI output port and most cards have some kind of audio metronome signal. Although some cards have more than one MIDI output connector, they can only address 16 MIDI channels, this means that the second (or third) output is simply an exact copy of the single MIDI output signal. These extra ports are the equivalent of MIDI THRU connectors found on the back of most synthesisers and are simply there for the convenience of connecting multiple sound modules onto the computer interface. Incidentally, Windows MPC soundcards that boast of 'MPU-401' compatibility almost invariably only implement a subset of the specification called UART or 'dumb' mode, an often fail to do this convincingly so should be avoided if you really need true MPU-401 compatibility.

MPU-401 shortcomings

The Roland design is a good hardware solution to the problem of interfacing a high speed MIDI data stream to a PC. However, the very nature of a hardware solution means that its specification is 'frozen'. Consequently the design cannot be improved to take advantage of any technical advances in the PC that have occurred since the card was released. As mentioned earlier, the MPU-401 card can't handle MIDI timecode (MTC) when used in intelligent mode, so tends to be used in 'dumb' or UART mode, which gives it little advantage over a simple serial port type interface.

Another shortcoming is that the MPU is limited to a tempo resolution of 192 pulses per quarter note (ppqn) whereas resolutions of 480 ppqn or higher are now commonly available in sequencers. To put this in context, at a tempo of 120 beats per minute (bpm), 192 ppqn will give you a timing resolution of just over 2.5 milliseconds whereas

480 ppqn will give a timing resolution of just over one millisecond. This difference is probably undetectable to most people, even to most professional musicians.

Research has shown that the timing resolution of the ear varies from 5 to 40 milliseconds depending on the type of sound, which is well above the resolution of both the above cases. The usual source of detectable MIDI delay is in the MIDI keyboard or sound module rather than the computer sequencer or MIDI chaining. Some early MIDI instruments had notoriously slow keyboard scan rates which led to sluggish response.

Research done by the authors into the response of certain synthesiser modules and samplers has shown delays of up to 20 milliseconds between the reception of the MIDI 'note on' message and the sound appearing at the audio outputs. The crucial consideration when considering these delays is whether they are constant or randomly variable. With a fixed delay the performer will automatically compensate – acoustic musicians do this as a matter of course, depending on their instrument. However an unpredictable delay will seriously foul up the 'feel' of the music unless it is somewhat less than the Haas limit – say five milliseconds.

External MIDI ports

Some PCs, such as laptop portable computers, don't have any ISA compatible internal expansion slots, so an internal MIDI interface card cannot be fitted. Another reason for not installing an interface internally is that you may wish to share the interface between several computers. To shift an interface based on an expansion card, you have to partially disassemble the computer, which can become tedious if you have to do it very often. Fortunately there are a number of MIDI interfaces that can be fitted externally to the PC.

As mentioned above, the problem with the PC serial port is not that it is too slow, but that it cannot be set to exactly 31,250 bits per second, which is the data rate needed for MIDI. This means that it is possible for the serial port to handle the amount of data, but not at the correct speed. A number of companies produce MIDI interfaces that overcome this problem in the form of external boxes that connect to one of the PC's serial ports. The facilities provided by these interfaces range from a single MIDI In and Out port to multi-port devices with full synchronisation facilities. The simpler devices can draw their power from the serial port while the rest usually need to have an external power supply.

Of course the serial port is not the only external connector found on the back of the PC, there is usually one or more parallel (or printer) ports which can be used for connecting MIDI devices to the PC. In some ways the printer port is more suitable for this purpose than the serial port since it doesn't have the same inherent speed restrictions. The downside is that not all parallel ports are created equal, in that some allow data to be read back – say for a MIDI In – while others don't. Like their serial brethren the interfaces range from a single port to multiple port devices, some with additional facilities like synchronisation.

Multi-port MIDI interfaces

When MIDI was designed, 16 channels controlling up to 16 independent instruments probably seemed more than enough. However due to the phenomenal success of MIDI, the number of MIDI synthesisers and MIDI-controlled effects units available has burgeoned. Couple this with the trend for multitimbral sound modules which use more than one MIDI channel, and it is now quite feasible for quite small MIDI set-ups to need more than 16 MIDI channels. This problem is exacerbated by certain other factors as well: guitar synthesisers usually allocate one MIDI channel per string, General MIDI synthesiser modules can use all 16 channels to simulate multiple acoustic instruments. While this is not usually a problem for live performance, sequencing systems can use lots of MIDI channels to allow the composer or song writer to simulate ensembles of instruments.

To get around this problem, more and more companies are developing MIDI interfaces with multiple MIDI outs. It is important here to appreciate the difference between MIDI THRUs and MIDI OUTs. A MIDI THRU is simply an exact copy of a MIDI IN and as such doesn't give you any more MIDI information, you can still only drive 16 instruments. The original Roland MPU-IPC card had two connectors labelled MIDI OUT connectors, but one of them was in fact a MIDI THRU, thus it had only 16 MIDI channels. The Music Quest MQX-32M card on the other hand, also has two MIDI OUTs but it can access 32 MIDI channels since each port is individually controllable.

Under DOS there was a problem with multi-port MIDI interfaces in that there wasn't much software available that supported more than a single port. Various card manufacturers addressed this problem by having an MPU-401 compatible mode, but this meant that you could not take full advantage of the multi-port facilities. However the advent of Windows 3.1 (with 'built-in' MIDI support) enabled manufacturers to provide an appropriate Windows driver to allow any Windows MIDI application to use the additional facilities. This also applies to synchronisation ports on the interface, since they can appear as a MIDI port that only receives or generates MIDI timecode (MTC).

MIDI on Windows MPC cards

The emergence of Windows as the most common operating environment for the PC has led to the popularity of the Multimedia PC (or MPC) soundcard. This incorporates MIDI into its specification in two ways. Firstly, these cards can be usually be used as a fairly basic MIDI interface, usually by the addition of a special cable that plugs into the card's joystick control port. Secondly the internal synthesiser found on these cards usually appears to the software as an external MIDI device. Hence you will usually find that a PC fitted with an MPC card will have both an internal MIDI port connected to the synthesiser as well as an 'external' MIDI port.

Most MPC soundcards have been developed from soundcards designed to be used for computer games and thus can be of rather suspect quality. This is especially true of soundcards based on the OPL3 FM synthesiser chipset, but thankfully these are being superseded by cards based on wavetable technology or the OPL4 chipset. Even so it is worth checking the specifications of any soundcard you plan to buy since other limitations can affect the usefulness of the card for music applications. Now that Windows is obviously here to stay, a number of the traditional pro-audio and musical instrument manufacturers have jumped onto the MPC bandwagon – producing soundcards with much higher quality than the games cards manufactures.

Sound modules with serial port interfaces

Up to this point we've only considered dedicated MIDI interfaces, i.e. those that don't perform any other function apart from communicating with external devices via MIDI or are fitted internally to the PC. There are however a growing band of synthesisers and sound modules that have a computer port as part of their specification. Yamaha started the trend with their TG100 GM sound module but similar products are now also available from Roland, Korg and various other manufacturers. From the MIDI point of view, these behave exactly like serial port interfaces mentioned above and are usually supplied with Windows driver software along with useful bundled software such as sequencers and MIDI file players (i.e. MIDI 'Juke boxes'). These can be a very cost-effective way of adding a music capability to a PC, especially for laptop users or those who want to shift their MIDI between PCs on a regular basis.

Figure 3.2 Korg's X5DR multitimbral sound module has an integral PC interface

Installing a MIDI interface or soundcard in your PC

Installing a MIDI interface or MPC soundcard in your PC can be a bit of a lottery to say the least. The problem is that the designers of the original PC didn't foresee the proliferation of expansion cards. They really didn't allow enough I/O addresses or interrupt lines for the number of cards that could be installed into each PC. This means that card designers have a rather limited choice, and it is quite common for two different cards to use the same address areas and interrupt lines. This situation gives rise to what's known as bus contention, which can give some very peculiar effects, as you can have two cards in a single PC that want to use the same address lines or interrupt.

In the main, internal MIDI cards require the use of only two system resources, an area of the I/O map's address space and an interrupt line (or IRQ). The 'standard' default value as originally defined by the Roland MPU-401 was interrupt 2 (i.e. IRQ 2) and address 330 hexadecimal. IRQ2 (also sometimes confusingly referred to as IRQ 9 or 2/9) is the first 'free' interrupt line, and thus tends to be used by other cards as well (for instance a SCSI card). This means that it is always a good idea to note in your PC's documentation the addresses and IRQ's your PC is actually using. Unless you happen to have a very old card you can usually alter both the I/O address and the IRQ number. If the default value doesn't work then it is simply a matter of experimenting with different settings until you find one that works.

MPC soundcards, on the other hand, usually need to use many more settings as they incorporate digital audio, a games joystick (or two) and quite possibly a CD-ROM interface. Since these cards need to use the PC's DMA (direct memory access) facility they can be quite complicated to get right. Some of the better ones can be configured via software, which can simplify the experimentation considerably, since you don't need to keep opening the PC to change the card's setting – usually using links (i.e. 'jumpers') or miniature switches on the expansion card. It is worthwhile ensuring that you tell the retailer what your PC's set-up is when you purchase a new expansion card to see if there are any known problems.

While the installation process can appear to be quite daunting, we have found that most sound and MIDI cards install with the default settings. Problems tend to occur when the PC either has a lot of cards installed or when two cards with overlapping functionality are fitted into the same PC. Remember that if all else fails you can always take the card back to the vendor and get a refund. Hopefully with the advent of the PCMIA bus and Windows 95's 'plug and play' facilities these problems will become a thing of the past.

Programming for MIDI

Virtually all the systems discussed above have technical information available that describes the software and hardware interface. The MPU-401 probably has the most information available, both for free from Roland and various on-line services and in the form of books. Music Quest also do a developer's pack for their range of products, which includes example source code and object libraries for various compilers. In Chapter 5 some different types of MIDI program are discussed with regard to developing your own software. These intimate details are only important if you are going to be writing software that directly accesses the card's hardware – say a DOS application. For Windows applications you can use the MIDI API calls provided by the operating system.

The most common computer language for professional MIDI application development on the PC is C, with time-critical code being written in assembler. There are several reasonably priced C compilers available, Borland's Turbo C probably being the most popular. There is also some work done in Pascal and the LPA Prolog MIDI extension is also worth a look if you want to have a go at artificial intelligence (AI) applications with MIDI. For an in-depth look at writing software for the MPU-401 interface (using C) the two books by Jim Conger are quite useful (see Appendix D). For smaller scale development, Microsoft's Visual Basic has proved to be popular, to the point that MIDI specific programming tools are available to help out the budding programmer.

MIDI interface examples

The rest of this chapter describes some common MIDI interfaces. This not meant to be a comprehensive list, rather a selection of different types to give you a feel for the various options available.

Roland interfaces

All Roland interfaces are MPU-401 compatible, this includes the MIDI interfaces found on their soundcards such as the SCC-1 and RAP-10. The original interface had all the connectors mounted on a metal box which was attached to the computer by a short ribbon cable. The current range seems to favour having mini-DIN sockets on the back plate of the card with short adapter cables to convert this to standard MIDI connectors. There is only one card that is 'MIDI Only' and even this has a connector that allows a synthesiser daughter board to be attached to the card (see Chapter 7 for more details).

Product details
MPU-401-AT
- 100% MPU-401 compatible (sic)
- half length expansion card
- MIDI connection via external adapter leads (supplied)
- Wide range of IRQ and port settings.
- Windows device driver included

The Voyetra interfaces

Voyetra have been around since the beginning of the MIDI revolution, producing what was arguably the first rack-mounted expander unit (i.e. a synthesiser without a keyboard) in the Voyetra 8 polyphonic synthesiser. They also produce MIDI software for the PC and a range of MIDI interface cards. Their original interfaces used the Roland MPU-401 chips so were totally compatible with the Roland specification, and of course any DOS software designed for the Roland interface when used in intelligent mode. Voyetra's current range of internal PC interfaces are not inherently MPU-401 compatible – and thus are not restricted by the MPU's limitations – but have the option of a daughter board that holds the Roland chipset to ensure 100% software compatibility with the MPU-401 standard. Voyetra also produce an external single port MIDI interface that fits onto the PC's parallel port.

There are two variants of the internal Voyetra interface – the V22 and the V24 which are both based around a common half-length card. The V22 has two MIDI INs and two OUTs which are connected to external synthesisers via four 'flying' leads. The V24 has a connector box on which are situated the MIDI connectors, the external SMPTE synchronisation connectors and a 'click' tempo input. The external connector box gives a very robust system suitable for professional situations and coupled with the timecode option makes it a suitable choice for professional applications.

V22 interface
- MPU-401 compatible with addition of daughter board
- 1/2 length expansion card
- two independent MIDI inputs
- two independent MIDI outputs
- no external synchronisation facilities (but can be upgraded to a V24)
- Windows device driver included (multi-client)

V24 interface
- MPU-401 compatible with addition of daughter board
- 1/2 length expansion card
- two independent MIDI inputs
- four independent MIDI outputs
- SMPTE/EBU timecode synchronisation
- 'click' tempo input
- MIDI connections via connector box
- Windows device driver included (multi-client)

V11 interface

- external unit (parallel port)
- not MPU-401 compatible
- buffered operation
- printer 'thru' port
- Windows device driver included (multi-client)

The Music Quest alternative

One company, Music Quest, have improved on the original Roland specification by producing an intelligent interface that is software compatible with the MPU-401 but doesn't use the Roland semiconductor chips. This has enabled Music Quest to put additional features on to their interface, such as improved synchronisation and additional MIDI ports, whilst allowing the use of normal MPU compatible software. Like Roland, Music Quest will provide details of the software interface to allow music program developers to take advantage of these additional features.

The extra features on Music Quest cards include multiple MIDI inputs and outputs, 'smart' FSK and full SMPTE and EBU timecode support. The range of cards starts with a basic MPU-401 compatible with no synchronisation and goes up to a dual MIDI port card with full timecode support. It is important to note that these extra (i.e. non-MPU) functions will be useful only with software that specifically supports the Music Quest cards.

Product details

PC MIDI card

- low cost MPU-401 compatible
- 1/3rd size expansion card
- MIDI metronome
- MIDI connection via adapter cable
- no synchronisation facilities
- Windows device driver included (multi-client)

Figure 3.3 Music Quest PC MIDI card

MQX-32M
- MPU-401 compatible
- 3/4 size expansion card
- unpitched metronome
- MIDI connection via adapter cable
- 'smart' FSK and SMPTE/EBU synchronisation
- supplied with utility and diagnostic disk
- two independent MIDI outputs
- two independent MIDI inputs
- Windows device driver included (multi-client)

Note: The non-MIDI signals are brought out to RCA phono jacks on the back plate of the card. The MIDI connections are to flying leads terminated in moulded plastic MIDI sockets.

MIDI Engine (8Port/SE, 2Port/SE, Note/1, Note/1+)
- not MPU-401 compatible
- fit to PC parallel port
- versions with 1, 2 and 8 MIDI input ports
- versions with 1, 2 and 8 MIDI output ports
- SMPTE/EBU synchronisation available on 8Port/SE and 2Port/SE units
- Windows device driver included (multi-client)

Key Electronics MIDIATOR

Key Electronics of Fort Worth, Texas produce a number of interfaces that can connect a PC to MIDI via its serial port. These interfaces perform a data rate conversion that matches a PC RS232 serial interface to the MIDI data stream. The MS-101 interface is a simple MIDI In/Out converter which draws its power from the PC's serial port, there is also a three port version which uses the unassigned pins on the MIDI sockets to provide the extra MIDI signals.

Product details

MS-101
- not MPU-401 compatible
- connects to PC serial port via cable
- no metronome
- MIDI connection via sturdy metal box
- no synchronisation facilities
- Windows device driver included

MS124
- not MPU-401 compatible
- connects to PC's serial port via cable
- no metronome
- MIDI connection via sturdy metal box
- one MIDI IN
- four MIDI OUTS
- Windows device driver included

Note: all the MIDIATOR serial interfaces are powered from the RS232 signal levels from the PC serial port. The MS-114 can also be powered from an auxiliary power supply.

MS128 (S/X/N)
- not MPU-401 compatible
- connects to PC's parallel port via cable
- no metronome
- MIDI connection via sturdy metal box
- two MIDI IN (S), one MIDI IN (N) or no MIDI IN (X)
- eight MIDI OUTS (S and X) or four MIDI OUTS (N)
- SMPTE/EBU synchronisation (S only)
- Windows device driver included

Purchase checklist

1 Ensure that the interface can be physically installed into your computer (i.e. check that you have spare slots, the bus type or port connector is correct etc.)
2 If it's an internal card, can it be configured to use different I/O addresses and interrupts (IRQ's).
3 Does it have much software available for it? Is it MPU-401 compatible? Does it come supplied with Windows drivers? Are they multi-client?
4 If you want to write MIDI programs, is there technical information available? Programmers' tool kit?
5 Does the card support multiple MIDI OUTs? Multiple MIDI THRUs?
6 Does the interface have any built-in tape synchronisation facilities? If so, does it support positional timecode? (refer to Chapter 5 for more details on this).
7 Does the card come with free or reduced cost software?
8 Does the card have an external metronome?
9 How mechanically robust are the connectors? For instance, flying MIDI leads with moulded DIN plugs might fail if you need to repeatedly change the MIDI connections in a 'live' situation.
10 How expensive is it?

MIDI sequencing on the PC

Using the computer as a sequencer is probably the most popular, rewarding, and most exciting use for computers in music. It effectively turns your computer into a tape recorder, but with many advantages over using conventional tape.

For the competent musician, using a sequencer offers increased flexibility, new possibilities when composing original works, and the chance to complete a work without having to use multitrack tape and expensive studio facilities. It also offers the non-musician the chance to discover music at his own pace, to experiment with instruments and harmonies and to achieve real results without any musical keyboard skills at all. The sequencer tells the user much about the interaction of instruments, how different sounds interrelate, classical and pop orchestration and arrangement, and about basic production techniques; what sounds good and what does not. It relies heavily on the use of the ear much more than on any technical musical ability or musical knowledge. Experiments with musical ideas are easy, and the rewards through playback are considerable. A sequencer is recommended to anyone interested in computers and music.

Sequencing has nothing specifically to do with computer generated sound, strange noises, modern electronic music, but everything to do with much of the music we hear daily. The sequencer is used extensively in pop music production, and when skilfully and intelligently used it may be impossible to tell whether the production involved 'live' players recorded on tape or computer-based sequencers.

Sequencers are often accused of producing lifeless monotonous music; such productions, if not deliberate, would be the fault of the operator or composer, not the sequencer itself. The sequencer is a friend to the musician and non-musician alike, and has become a crucial asset to most music production. The only real criticism against the technology is that it sometimes reduces the number of live musicians used in a project. Even so, one often finds that the drummer is the one who programs the drum patterns into the sequencer, and the bass player programs the bass.

A sequencer is a computer program – a bit like a word processor – that stores a musical performance in the computer's memory. You can then edit the music in the same way that you would manipulate the characters in a document, except that instead of letters you are manipulating notes. You can then play it back using a MIDI sound module, just as with a word processor you would print it out using a printer. Now if you want get the best out of your word processor you need to know the capabilities of your printer. Likewise, before we can explain the features and facilities offered by a sequencer, we first need to look at its operating environment.

The MIDI environment

As we have seen in Chapter 3, instruments with a MIDI implementation give out digital data through their MIDI OUT socket when played. The computer, running sequencing software, will record this in relation to time, store it and be ready to send it back out to the instrument on the play command from the user. The MIDI information, when sent back out from the computer either to the soundcard or to the MIDI IN socket on the instrument, will remotely play the notes that the performer played note for note with the original rhythm and 'touch'.

Thus if you have one MIDI keyboard and a computer with a MIDI interface running sequencing software, the most basic configuration would be to attach the keyboard to the computer using both MIDI IN and OUT sockets, so that it can send MIDI to the computer and receive MIDI back from the computer. Put the sequencer into record, play your keyboard, stop recording, locate the first bar, press play and your instrument will be told to produce through MIDI exactly what you played – just like a tape recorder. The sequencer will record (or has the option to record) everything you play, including the velocity of the notes as you play (how hard you hit them), the sustain pedal, any pitch bend or modulation that you use, any different sounds that you select while playing. The resulting playback from the computer will be an exact reproduction of your performance.

The first advantage over tape recording is already apparent; rather than having a recording of a performance, we have a live re-performance of the piece. Thus there will be no sound quality degradation, no tape hiss, noise, distortion, drop-outs, and no coughs or distractions in the background. Essentially we have the original performance again produced to the same quality. So much for those rumours about sequencers only being able to produce static, expressionless music, since using a sequencer in this way merely reproduces the original. It also illustrates how a sequencer does not favour a particular style of music. The sequencer does not know (or care) about the music it records, it simply remembers the MIDI events as they happen, stores them, and on command, replays them through the attached instrument.

The sequencer in your MIDI set-up

The sequencer program on your computer will always be at the heart of your MIDI set-up since it has the task of controlling all the instruments. It has the capability of talking to many pieces of equipment at the same time all down one MIDI lead by using the MIDI channel system (see Appendix A). In professional studios the sequencer will often be controlling sound generation equipment plus sound processing equipment (reverberation units, etc.), and sometimes the mixing desk itself by providing mix automation.

Daisy chaining sound modules

As the sequencer has to be able to talk to all MIDI equipment, it requires connection to each item. There are three ways to connect your MIDI system, although each method can be mixed with the others as your set-up demands; one uses the THRU sockets on your MIDI equipment, the other a separate THRU box, and the third uses a multi-port computer MIDI interface. By using the THRU sockets, additional keyboards, drum machines, or other MIDI equipment can be chained together so that they all receive the same information. The THRU socket on each device sends out a duplicate of information received at the IN socket. This is sometimes called 'daisy chaining'. (Figure 4.1).

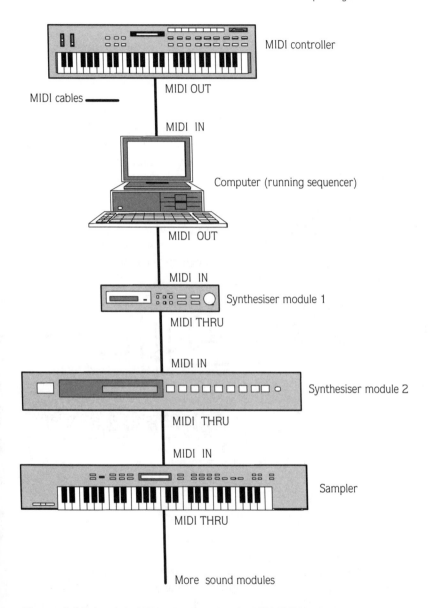

MIDI controller

MIDI cables ▬▬

MIDI OUT

MIDI IN

Computer (running sequencer)

MIDI OUT

MIDI IN

Synthesiser module 1

MIDI THRU

MIDI IN

Synthesiser module 2

MIDI THRU

MIDI IN

Sampler

MIDI THRU

More sound modules

Figure 4.1 Daisy chain MIDI network using the MIDI THRU sockets

Star network

While it is convenient to simply link the MIDI THRU of each synthesiser to the IN of the next one down the line, it means you must
switch all the modules on, which might be a bit troublesome if you just
want to use the last one in the chain. Therefore, it is worth getting an
inexpensive MIDI THRU box. This will allow multiple MIDI THRU ports
from the same box, which can feed each instrument separately. This is
called a 'star' network with each unit being at a point of the star and
your computer with THRU box being at the hub or centre of the star.
(Figure 4.2)

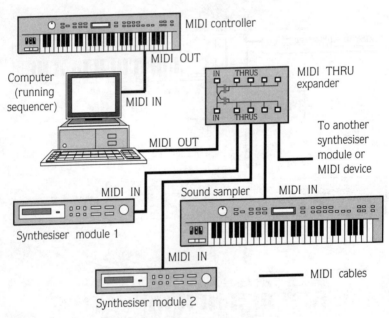

Figure 4.2 Star network using MIDI THRU expander

Multi-port interface

The third option is to use a multi-port MIDI interface with your
computer, and a sequencer program that will support it. This option
gives you more MIDI channels than the other two, as each separate
port has 16 channels. Multitimbral sound modules are capable of playing separate instruments on all 16 channels; because of this, and the

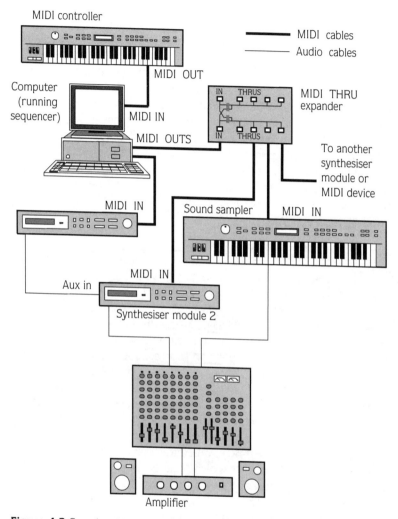

Figure 4.3 Complete MIDI sequencing system to give a tapeless MIDI studio

convenience of keeping equipment such as MIDI mixing desks on a separate MIDI port, this third option is particularly useful. Figure 4.3 shows a MIDI set-up using all three methods of MIDI connection.

The MIDI data for a sequence is sent to the MIDI IN of the computer from the instrument you wish to physically play. This may be a 'controller keyboard' – that is a keyboard that makes no sound on its own but controls other sound generators by sending out MIDI data or any other MIDI equipped instrument. Thus the computer sits in between the instrument you play, and the instruments providing the sounds (which may of course be the same instrument). The controlling instrument that sends the MIDI information does not have to be a keyboard, there are MIDI wind instruments, guitars and drums, as well as mixing desks, pedals, even microphone systems all of which send out MIDI information. The program will be able to relay the information received on its MIDI interface IN socket to the OUT socket to play the sounds. In this position, the sequencer can monitor and record (if asked to) everything you perform, and (without reconnection) can tell the instruments making the sounds when and what to play.

Audio connections

The other connections you will have to make to complete your MIDI studio set-up are the audio outputs of your sound generators. This includes the audio output from your soundcard if you have one installed. The audio output from your synthesiser (or expander module) will either be built-in (usually speakers inside the keyboard) or will need amplifying by a hi-fi system or musical instrument amplifier. If you intend to have more than two sound sources, you will need to address the problem of mixing the outputs of the sound modules before amplification. The best way to handle this would be to buy a small audio mixer or – if you are lucky – you'll be able to use external inputs on one of the instruments (see Figure 4.3) which are sometimes provided for this purpose.

On older type MPU-401 MIDI interfaces, a metronome output was available from the card that also required amplification. Most modern sequencer programs have the option either to use the 'beep' of the PC speaker, or to generate a MIDI click, which is programmable to play a percussion sound on your soundcard or MIDI equipment. The ability to hear and then play along with the metronome in some form, is important, otherwise bar by bar editing functions and staff notation in the sequencer will be meaningless.

Producing the sounds

The capacity of your MIDI set-up to create large scale compositions using different sounds, is usually limited only by the instrument, or instruments, that are producing the sound. You will usually find that any sequencer program will be more than able to control all your sound modules. However, if your one keyboard can play only one sound at a time (piano or flute or trumpet, etc.), then no matter what you do, the sequencer will be able to play only one sound, and all your compositions, regardless of how many sequencer tracks are available, will all be single sound. Similarly a single soundcard limits your compositions to the sounds offered by that card.

It is therefore important to be aware of the capabilities of the MIDI equipment and soundcards which you will be using with your sequencer, as this will give you a good idea of the scope of composition that will be possible. The two crucial specifications to look for on your keyboard, sound module or soundcard are the polyphony and its multitimbral capability.

Polyphony

Polyphony indicates the maximum number of notes, regardless of the sound, that the instrument is capable of producing at the same time. Thus if you call up a piano sound, and rest your fore-arm on the keys, pressing them all down, a certain number will sound, the rest won't. All sound generators have a specification for polyphony; keyboards, modules, soundcards. For example, the Roland JV1080 rackmount synthesiser has a polyphony of 64, the Yamaha P-series pianos has 32, the Korg M1 has 16 and the Casio CZ101has 8. Similarly for soundcards; the Advanced Gravis Ultrasound and Ensoniq Soundscape cards include a 32 note (or voice) synthesiser, the Amitek Jazz 16 has a 20 voice synth, and the SoundBlaster Pro has an 18 voice type.

Nearly all sequencer programs are capable of sending out 128 note chords on all 16 MIDI channels, that's a total of 2048 notes simultaneously down one MIDI cable – don't be surprised if your home keyboard when presented with all these notes to play, gives up and sounds only eight.

Multitimbral capability

The other important specification is the instrument's multitimbral capability. This determines how many different sounds (piano, bass, trumpet, drums, etc.) can play at the same time. It is only relatively recently that this has become important, and it is solely due to the increase in use of sequencers. The original Yamaha DX7 keyboard had no multitimbral capability – you selected a sound, played it, selected a different one, and played that, there was no way either on the keyboard, or through MIDI that two could play simultaneously. On a multitimbral instrument the different sounds are accessed using different MIDI channels, so that sending two Middle C notes, one on channel 1 and one on channel 2 could play two different sounds on the same instrument at the same time. It is this specification that allows a sequencer to play a bass-line, piano line, and drum-kit simultaneously. Sound modules such as the Roland CM300, CM500, and E-mu Proteus have a multitimbral capability of 16 selectable sounds. Other examples are the Korg M1, which is eight sound (or part) multitimbral and the Yamaha P series pianos that are two part multitimbral.

On a multitimbral instrument you are able to select which sound you want to play for a particular channel. The sound is called up by a MIDI program change message sent by the sequencer (see Appendix A), which corresponds to pushing one of the sound select buttons on the front panel of a keyboard. So while your soundcard or sound module might be only eight voice multitimbral, you have a whole list of sounds from which to choose the eight. If this is confusing, take the time to look through the paragraphs below, as it may avoid disappointment when you hook up your keyboard or sound module to your sequencer.

Instrument list

A keyboard, module or soundcard will boast a list of sounds that it can produce; trumpet, piano, strings, drums, organ, harpsichord, etc. The list is usually impressive, but when used with a sequencer this is only one of three important specifications. A General MIDI or GM compatible instrument (or instrument that has a 'GM set' among its sounds) will have a specific list of sounds assigned to program numbers in a special order. The introduction of the GM specification aimed to standardise sounds called up by MIDI, and is essential when sharing MIDI files with people who probably won't have the same equipment as you.

Polyphony or number of voices

The polyphony of the keyboard indicates the maximum number of notes that can sound at the same time, or effectively the maximum number of notes in a chord. On a multitimbral instrument this number is split between the different sounds accessed on different MIDI channels. The polyphony is sometimes documented as 'voice' (e.g. a 32 voice synthesiser).

Multitimbral features

This is the number of different sounds that can play simultaneously and completely independently of each other. This has nothing to do with split keyboards, since true multitimbral instruments have all notes available to different sounds. Depending on your instrument you may have to switch it into a multitimbral mode, and then create your own selection of instruments to respond on each MIDI channel. On soundcards and 'computer music' sound modules the set-up is already in place, and simply requires the sequencer program to send the different program numbers on each MIDI channel to call up the required sounds.

Knowing the total polyphony and multitimbral capabilities of your MIDI equipment, will ensure you get the best from your sequencing software.

The MPC soundcard

The MPC soundcard provides the neat option of having a sound source within the PC running Windows. Modern multimedia upgrade packs offer soundcards, CD ROM drives and a set of speakers all in one box; if you buy the soundcard on its own you'll need to amplify the card through your hi-fi or with a set of small speakers; otherwise you'll be forced to wear headphones all the time! The soundcard will have the option to add a MIDI interface, this will usually be quite basic, and you may find you require an additional MIDI interface card for your PC if you want to use external timecode synchronisation, audio trigger input, or multi-port features.

If you've installed your soundcard for Windows and intend to run a Windows sequencer program then you'll be able to choose whether to play the sounds on the soundcard or use sounds in external MIDI equipment by routing tracks to the MIDI interface on the soundcard. The sounds included on the card may or may not be adequate for your musical compositions, and rather than upgrading your card each time, the MIDI interface provides the means to expand your available sounds.

Also you need to remember that if you want to play your music into the sequencer from a MIDI keyboard, you'll need to use the MIDI interface to be able to connect your MIDI keyboard. This is actually a far quicker way of getting the 'notes' in to the computer than using the step-time entry from the computer. Most MPC soundcards require a special cable – connected to the card's games port – to give access to the built in MIDI ports. Be sure to go to a reputable dealer to get this MIDI add-on, as these cables are notoriously unreliable and often do not work as advertised.

Sequencer basics

Computer sequencers offer many advantages over traditional audio tape recording techniques. There is no rewind or fast forward time; you can record and playback without sound degradation or worrying about tape quality, tape speed variation, or the number of times you record over old recordings attempting to get the piece correct. More important if you make a mistake, you can correct it without having to re-record, by simply finding the offending note or notes in the sequencer edit pages, and correcting them individually. You can also record at slower tempos and then speed up the playback without changing the pitch. You can input notes one by one without having to play in time, and then ask the computer to work out the timing, tempo and rhythm; or you can play in the easy sections of your piece, and then step-enter the difficult passages. Sections can be transposed, cut, copied, deleted, repeated, inverted all through on-screen operations.

The sequencer is often presented as a type of multitrack tape recorder, where individual recordings are made on separate tracks. These tracks then play back together. In our original example of putting the sequencer into record, playing, and then getting the sequencer to play back, we were using just one track. To further build a piece, new tracks can be recorded while listening back to others, so for example, track 2 is in record while track 1 plays back; then tracks 1 and 2 play back while track 3 records, and so on. The different tracks can be assigned to play different sounds, and named accordingly: track 1 – piano, track 2 – bass, track 3 – brass. This example assumes that your sound modules are multitimbral.

The relationship (and difference) between tracks and channels can often cause confusion, so to summarise; MIDI allows 16 separate channels, and it is therefore possible to control 16 different polyphonic sounds or instruments using a sequencer with one MIDI output port. However, a sequencer may boast 100s of tracks all free and available for recording MIDI data. All this means is that the user has the option to keep data separate, even though its destination may be a single instrument or sound. For instance you may wish to have the chorus bass line on a different track to the verse bass line. Both tracks use the same MIDI channel, and play the same sound, but keeping the tracks separate allows you to do track editing operations (e.g. increase the volume, transpose, stereo pan, mute or solo, etc.) on the verse and chorus independently. Similarly you may have the whole drum kit spread on different notes up and down the keyboard all available though one MIDI channel.

There are considerable advantages in using a different track of the sequencer for each drum, so that if a section of your piece required no tambourine, you can simply mute one track, rather than trying to edit out the tambourine note from one track containing all the other drums and percussion. Spreading your work over a greater number of tracks gives increased control over your music, and speeds editing.

Quantising

There are certain features common to all sequencers. The ability to edit individual events or notes is essential and is discussed fully in the following section. Quantising is a common feature, that enables the timing correction of playing. The process shifts notes onto beats or fractions of beats, so that everything sits correctly in time. While quantising is one of the most important sequencer features, its careless use can easily produce lifeless, mechanical music. To illustrate quantising imagine playing middle C repeatedly, as fast as you can (or if you read music playing the excerpt in Figure 4.4).

Figure 4.4 Example of a musical phrase for quantising

If you record this on your sequencer, and then quantise to quarter notes, (four divisions of a semibreve, i.e. crotchets) the sequencer will play back notes on the beat – not ignoring the others, but simply shifting them to the nearest beat – Figure 4.5(a). Quantising to 8ths will shift notes to the nearest quaver beat – Figure 4.5(b).

Figure 4.5(a) Example after quantising to quarter notes

Figure 4.5(b) Example after quantising to eighth notes

The quantisation capabilities will vary from package to package but most will also have triplet units, and a fine resolution of 64ths of a semibreve or higher. If no quantisation is applied, then your recording will be at the resolution of the program. This specification shows how fine the software can resolve or quantise notes within a beat. e.g. the resolution of Cubase Score is 384ppq (pulses per quarter note) – related to time that's a resolution of just over 1.3 milliseconds at 120 bpm.

The basic functions of different sequencer programs are very similar, although their approach, layout and editing options often vary considerably. Most sequencers adopt a linear approach to recording while most drum machines and some auto-accompaniment software use a pattern-based system.

In a linear sequencer, tracks and songs are recorded on a continuous scale of increasing bars, thus at the end of a composition the final bar may be 300 or more. Rather than playing the piece in its entirety, the copy and paste functions allow sections to be copied and inserted into their correct position. For example if you record an eight bar verse followed by an eight bar chorus, and then require the second verse to be followed by two choruses, then you would copy the first eight bars (the first verse) and insert them after the first chorus, then copy the chorus twice and paste those 16 bars on the end. The piece would then play verse, chorus, verse, chorus, chorus.

Drum machines and pattern-based sequencers (rare) create songs by stringing together sections (or patterns) one after another. So for our example above we would have recorded two patterns:

Pattern 1   8 bar verse
Pattern 2   8 bar chorus

Our song would then be written by programming the sequencer to compile the following play list

1   1 x pattern 1
2   1 x pattern 2
3   1 x pattern 1
4   2 x pattern 2

No actual copying of data is necessary. This is obviously a very quick way to construct a piece of music, since each pattern only has to be created once. The only problem with this is that the human ear (or mind) is very good at recognising repetition. The result of this is that music that incorporates a large amount of repetition will sound flat and lifeless – or in other words 'boring'.

Obviously the same applies to the linear sequencing example above after the verses and choruses have been copied, but since each of these new copies is a new set of MIDI data, they can be individually edited to add variation. There is one advantage of using a pattern-based sequencer which is that changing one note in the pattern will change it throughout out the entire sequence. This can be very handy under certain circumstances, especially during the early stages of the development of a piece of music.

Ghost parts

Some linear sequencers – Cubase for instance – have a kind of halfway house in the ability to create 'ghost' parts. Creating a ghost part is similar to the linear copy/paste example above except that no new data is created. At playback, the sequence will simply refer back to the original data when it reaches a ghost. This means that any changes in the original data – say due to an edit – will be reflected in any ghosts throughout the rest of the sequence.

Ghost parts can usually be converted into a normal linear tracks by altering the data using one of the sequencer's built-in editors. This means that a sequencer that can create ghost parts can give the best of both worlds, the only problem is that you can easily lose track of which parts are 'real' and which are ghosts.

The record time – or the maximum length of a song – that a sequencer can handle is usually dependent on how much MIDI data is in the piece. For example if the sequencer has a capacity of 60,000 notes, then, at a tempo of 120bpm, in a piece composed entirely of single crotchets, the sequencer could hold a piece lasting 8 hours and 20 minutes! If however during the same piece someone (possibly a toddler in the house) was continuously waggling the pitch bend lever on the side of the keyboard while you played, you'd be lucky to get 15 minutes of recording time, due to the huge amount of MIDI data generated by a pitch wheel movement. It is thus impossible to give a specification for the recording time for a sequencer but the capacity in MIDI events is a useful measure.

Sequencer programs for Windows rarely have problems with memory, and there are usually indicators showing available free memory, although loading large system exclusive dumps can sometimes present problems (see Appendix A for an explanation of MIDI system exclusive).

Editing

Sequencer programs offer a number of formats for editing music. These can be summarised as four main types:

1   Track editor (overview)
2   Staff notation
3   Grid or piano roll
4   Event listing

An increasing number of sequencer programs offer all four editing screens, and the user can decide which format suits best. Programs with less than four edit screens usually leave out staff notation and/or event listing.

Track editor

This screen provides an overview of the work (Figure 4.6). It shows multiple tracks and multiple bars and can be scrolled and sized to see more or less of the piece. The track status is displayed – the MIDI channel, sound name, solo, mute, looping, record ready, etc. From this screen, larger sections of music can be edited, for example, copying the first four bars of all the tracks, or quantising the eight bars of the chorus on the drums, percussion and bass tracks.

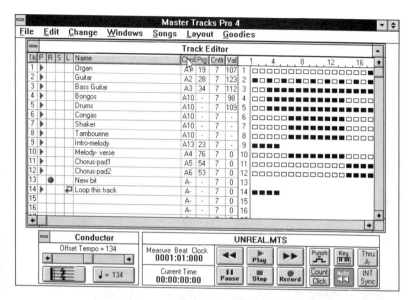

Figure 4.6 Track editor in Mastertracks Pro4

Programs such as Steinberg's Cubase allow data areas to be named rather than just appearing as dots, this further provides a useful visual overview of your music – the chorus is instantly recognisable because the block has been named 'chorus'!

Event editing screens

Editing notes and other MIDI events within a bar requires a more detailed view, and here there is the choice of format; grid view, event listing or staff notation. To give an example of the three types of editing display imagine playing the first four notes of the scale of C starting on middle C playing on the beat in crotchets.

If you were a PERFECT player the three types of editing screen would look like Figure 4.7 (a), (b) and (c).

Note how all the notes start on the beat and are exactly a crotchet beat in length.

Figure 4.7 Three edit screens with crotchets in time
(a) Grid view

Figure 4.7 Three edit screens with crotchets in time
(b) Event listing

Figure 4.7 Three edit screens with crotchets in time
(c) Staff notation

However very few people can play such perfect crotchets in real-time, and usually notes are held on a fraction too long, or cut off too short. The result therefore is more likely to be like Figure 4.8.

Figure 4.8 The same three screens with the likely result of actual playing (a) Grid view

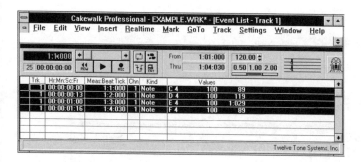

Figure 4.8 The same three screens with the likely result of actual playing (b) Event listing

Figure 4.8 The same three screens with the likely result of actual playing (c) Staff notation

If you then wished to add a crotchet G over the E, then the three edit screens may look like this: (Figure 4.9 a, b, c)

Notice how the musical notation screen is becoming increasingly difficult to read as it attempts to display the correct notation for the bar. The grid edit screen retains a recognisable pattern, while the event list faithfully reproduces the accurate list of note start times and durations, but does not give any sort of 'feel' of how the note will sound.

Figure 4.9 (a) Grid view with added G

Figure 4.9 (b) Event listing with added G

Figure 4.9 (c) Staff notation with added G

The examples show how unfriendly musical notation can be when trying to edit a real-time performance (see the discussion in Chapter 2 on real-time scoring), and the user must consider the benefits and disadvantages of using a musical notation editing option. It should also be noted that some sequencers will automatically 'quantise' the notation editing display to make it look more 'musical'. However, as this means that the displayed notation no longer reflects the actual underlying note data, it becomes of limited use when you need to start editing the notes.

To go back to the word processor analogy, it's as if you had a spelling checker that corrected the spelling on the screen display but still output the spelling mistakes to the printer. Some sequencers simply allow the display of notation but require that you use one of the other editors to alter the data.

Editing on the three screens involves either changing the parameters of a displayed event, or deleting, inserting or copying items; in the event list, items are changed by simply typing in a new value – thus C4 can be changed to D4 (a tone up), and the velocity of the note changed to any value between 1 and 128.

On both the grid edit and notation edit screens, notes can be graphically deleted, inserted and copied, and information about the dynamics of the note changed either graphically or using text, by calling up information about the note. Additional MIDI events, such as program changes, or controller events (e.g. sustain pedal), recorded on that particular track, are shown elsewhere on this or another screen. In the event list all MIDI data is listed in time order.

So through a combination of editing on a large scale, where groups of bars can be modified, and on a small scale that gives access to individual events, compositions are constructed and modified after an initial recording. Individual notes and additional events can be added in step-time (i.e. without going back into record) on the edit pages.

For editing other MIDI data, programs may have other dedicated screens, or make use of an area within an existing one. For instance, to edit pitch bend or modulation wheel data on Passports Mastertracks Pro4 you have the option to draw data as shown in Figure 4.10.

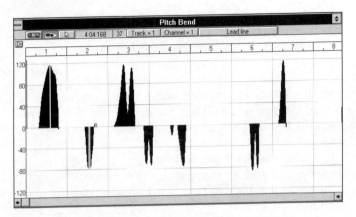

Figure 4.10 Pitch bend editing on Mastertracks Pro 4

Synchronisation

Synchronising the playback of your music to other external equipment allows integration into a larger music studio. All but the most basic of sequencers will synchronise to other MIDI sequencers and drum machines by using Song Position Pointer messages (SPP) and MIDI clock. This sends timing clock and song position information using the same MIDI cable as all the note data, and it allows MIDI equipment to start, pause and continue, and locate the correct bar and beat within the song, all in synchronisation with each other.

Non-MIDI equipment such as tape machines, VCRs, Portastudios require synchronisation using timecode; either as longitudinal timecode (LTC – often referred to as SMPTE) which can be recorded as an audio code on a tape, or as MIDI timecode (MTC) – the MIDI equivalent. To read and synchronise to MTC your software must specifically have this option, and in addition MTC is often a direct conversion from existing LTC.

To read and synchronise to LTC you will need a computer MIDI interface that supports timecode input, and a program that supports the interface! For further discussion on synchronisation and MIDI interfaces see Chapter 3.

A few sequencers (for instance Cakewalk Windows and Cubase Score) also support MIDI machine control (MMC). Tape machines equipped with MMC capability are able to have their transport controlled by MIDI data from the sequencer program, so that the software,

Figure 4.11 The Alesis ADAT XT. Combining an ADAT with a SoundScape hard disk recorder gives you the best of both worlds

although slaving to timecode once the tape machine is playing, will appear to be a master machine; i.e. pressing the play button on your sequencer will also start your tape machine.

Current MMC-equipped tape machines include the digital eight track recorders; Alesis ADAT (with either AI-2 synchronisation box, BRC remote controller, JLC DataSync2 or Steinberg ACI), Tascam DA88, Fostex RD8, and the later Fostex analogue multitrack recorders.

Even if synchronisation is not required, a composer may wish to relate the composition to real-time (hours, minutes, seconds). For example, composers for film and video soundtrack receive a list of important cues in the piece, and need to match them with musical events. In this instance, a sequencer working in bars and beats at given tempos, does not help the composer locate a position at say 4 minutes 32 seconds from the start. If the program includes a real-time analysis feature then it can calculate time positions in the piece based on the tempo and display these in hours, minutes, seconds, frames corresponding to timecode standard.

Windows multimedia events

Within the Windows environment MIDI is just one of the options available under the general heading of multimedia. Some Windows sequencer programs include the facilities to sequence other multimedia events by including MCI (Media Control Interface) commands. MCI commands allow the control of various multimedia devices under Windows, such as the control and playback of .WAV audio files, CD audio, animation and video. For the computer musician the ability to

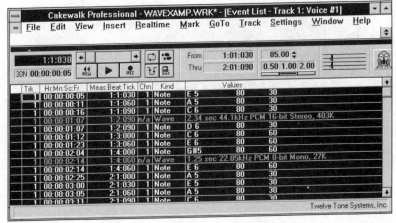

Figure 4.12 Embedded MCI .WAV play command

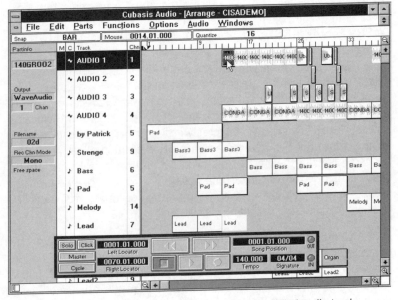

Figure 4.13 Cubasis Audio Arrange window showing digital audio tracks

play back .WAV audio files is probably the most useful. These are 'real' audio extracts and could for example be the complete vocal part that accompanies the MIDI sequence, or perhaps some special sound effects missing from available MIDI equipment.

Both Cakewalk Windows, and Mastertracks Pro4 use the event list to insert and edit MCI events (they'd be difficult to display in staff notation!). Figure 4.12 shows a .WAV file playback command embedded within a bar of MIDI data.

More advanced 'audio' variants of popular sequencing packages – like Cubase Audio – allow the waveforms to be displayed in the track overview window (Figure 4.13). Further discussion and information on Windows multimedia is included in Chapter 6.

Taming the sequencer

It seems slightly ironic that having used the computer to accurately record our music, we then introduce features that will 'humanise' the music again. It's a bit like asking your word processor to randomly misspell a few words to make the text a bit more human! Still, it's true that computer-generated sequences can easily sound stilted, boring, and without what we might call musicality. This is particularly true when step-entry methods have been used; that is inserting individual notes onto the editing screens one by one. All the notes are exactly on the beat, exactly the correct length, and all have the same velocity. The sequencer has the dual task of tidying up our human input – played from MIDI equipment, and un-tidying the computer-generated input.

Many sequencers feature a percentage quantise function, so that rather than shifting notes on to the beat, it shifts them a percentage closer to the beat. This means, for example, that applying an increasing percentage triplet quantise to a section of music will gradually add a 'swing' to the piece.

More interesting is groove quantise – now offered on a number of sequencers. Grooves are timing patterns or templates either pre-set in the software, loaded from disk files, or created by analysing a part of your own sequence. Grooves are applied to areas of your music in the same manner as quantising, and can be useful in applying a 'style' to a piece. In addition to timing, a groove can also contain analysed information about the relative velocities of the notes, so that accents are also applied.

73

Other programs offer a randomising function which, when applied to note start times and velocities, can rid a track of an inflexible beat. Applying randomisation to note pitches can help the composer stuck for ideas!

Tempo control can also be useful in humanising sequences. Programs allow tempo variation by using a tempo map that runs alongside the music controlling the tempo. Editing can be graphical or text-based and tempo changes can be instant or gradual over a section.

Global editing

The editing screens shown in Figures 4.7 to 4.9 are useful for editing specific MIDI events; the pitch of a note, a program change, an MCI playback command. Global editing functions allow changes of a specific kind to be made over defined areas of the piece. Adjusting individual parameters of notes or MIDI events over long sections of a track is extremely tedious if it has to be done note by note; for instance to increase the note velocities for eight bars to give a crescendo, would otherwise mean editing individual notes for the complete area. With global editing, an increasing note velocity is automatically assigned to all notes within a specified section. Similarly if you wish to change the snare drum used on your track, the global editing functions will search out all instances of a specified note on single or multiple tracks, delete, and replace them with notes of a different pitch (e.g. to play a different snare drum sound).

Editing filters further expand editing power by isolating events from others for editing. For example the accents within a track can be further exaggerated by adding a percentage increase to notes whose velocities are already over 90. Another example is the ability to strip out the left hand part from a piano track, by deleting all notes below C3.

The possibilities for change and refinement using global editing are enormous, such editing power is essential when one considers that everyone enters music in different styles, has different playing abilities, and is expecting a different end-result in playback.

Advanced options

We have seen the basic features of a sequencer; in addition many sequencers boast extra features to aid editing, and enhance the MIDI control. A few of these options that are of particular interest are outlined below:

Harmonic transposition

While a normal transposition will change the key of a composition, or part of a composition, a harmonic transposition will take into account the key of the piece, and transpose accordingly. This method is useful for obtaining harmonies for melody lines. For those needing a musical example, transposing the scale of C major up 4 semitones will give you the scale of E major, harmonically transposing the scale of C up the same amount with the key set to C major will give you the scale of C starting on E (i.e. no F#, G#, C# or D#). Programs such as Voyetra's Sequencer Plus Gold also offer harmonic transposition based on both key and mode (Dorian, Phrygian, etc.).

System exclusive (or SysEx)

The way in which sequencers handle system exclusive (or SysEx) data varies between programs. There may be the option either to include the SysEx messages within a track, or to send them as discrete data before the track starts. Track embedded SysEx messages, can be useful to change some of the more obscure features within a synthesiser that are not accessible through standard MIDI controller commands while the sequencer is playing. SysEx messages can also cause problems because they cannot be interrupted or interleaved with other note or controller data. This makes it impossible to send large messages within a track without playback faltering. It is usually left to the person using the sequencer to leave a large enough gap in the music to ensure that the message does not interfere with normal MIDI data. Other sequencers have a specific area of the program, usually called a librarian, that handles SysEx transfer. It is usually possible to relate librarian files to sequence files, so that the program will load all files related to a particular song.

It should be noted that the original MIDI specification didn't contemplate the possibility of large SysEx transmissions being interleaved with live performance data. The upshot of this is that MIDI has no mechanism for handling the delays that might be caused and it is up to the composer to ensure that there are no unwanted side-effects when large SysEx dumps are inserted in a MIDI sequence.

Drum editing

A few programs offer a special editing screen for drum and percussion tracks. When triggering drum sounds the length of the MIDI note is usually irrelevant since the sounds will play the full length of their 'sample'. This is reflected in the editing page, where graphics for single hits replace note blocks. Figure 4.14 shows the drum editing screen from Cakewalk. Notice that using instrument templates (e.g. GM set drums) means that the program can automatically name the sound on each pitch.

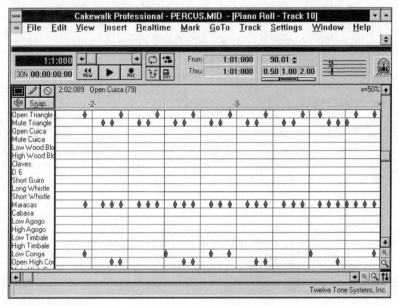

Figure 4.14 Drum editing screen in Cakewalk

Loop in record

Loop in record is a function familiar to drum machine programmers. A loop is set in the sequencer – maybe two or four bars, and while recording, notes can be continually added to the bars in the loop. For example, to record a four bar drum sequence, the program can loop in record every four bars; on the first pass you play the bass drum, on the second pass you add the snare, etc., until the full kit is recorded in the four bars. The four bars can then be copied out to suit the song.

Automatic tempo assign

Rather than playing along to a tempo set by the computer through the metronome it produces, it may be possible to let the sequencer listen to a tap you make through a MIDI controller or note while you are playing the piece. In this way after the recording the sequencer can correctly assign notes within the bars. In systems that have a special MIDI interface it is possible to provide the sequencer with an external audio click — it could be a metronome or the hi-hat from 'live' drums on tape; useful if you wanted to add sequenced MIDI percussion to a live drum track.

Instruments and GM/GS

General MIDI (GM) sets out specifications for synthesisers and includes a list of sounds on specific MIDI program numbers. Roland's GS specification takes this further with standards for different banks of sounds and additional parameters such as reverb and chorus control. Using GM compatible sequencers allows you to choose the named sound for your track and the program will know which MIDI program change number to send. Some programs extend this principle and provide a list of synthesisers, tone modules and soundcards in addition to GM equipment, with program maps for each. GM equipment also has a standardised set of MIDI controllers to affect functions such as MIDI volume and pan position, so you may find that your program has dedicated controls for these.

MIDI mixing

Automated mixing has until recently been left to large expensive computer-controlled mixing consoles. Today, an increasing number of medium-priced mixers have a MIDI implementation. This may be simple channel mute functions, or it could be full automation including fader control. Sequencer programs such as Cakewalk include a fully assignable mixing page, which allows control of a range of external MIDI equipment including MIDI desks while the sequencer is running. So changing the screen position of buttons, knobs and faders sends out user-programmed MIDI data — i.e. to affect the mix in some way. The option to have these changes recorded gives a fully automated mix saved with the music sequence file.

Sequencers with a difference

Programs like Jammer, Superjam and Band in a Box are essentially sequencers that include a selection of pre-programmed styles — a bit like home keyboards with rhythm selections. The styles (jazz, dance, hip-hop, big-band) can be played by instrument ensembles of your choice, and the chord sequences can be loaded from files or user-programmed. All that's left is for you to 'jam' along with them. These types of program are excellent for improving playing technique and for learning about different music styles. There are also sequencers which provide alternatives to the standard keyboard-oriented user interface. For instance the PowerChords Sequencer from Howling Dog Systems is based around a guitar fretboard rather than a piano-style keyboard.

Purchase checklist

1 Make sure the program will run on your computer. Check memory, disk and video card requirements, and whether the program requires Windows.
2 The program will require some kind of MIDI interface or sound-card. Make sure there are no problems in fitting this in your computer (lap-tops may not have an expansion slot.) Also micro-channel computers require special MCA compatible expansion cards which are both rare and expensive. Windows sequencers will work with any Windows compatible soundcard, but you may require an add-on MIDI interface if you want to input music from a MIDI keyboard and output MIDI to external equipment.
3 Make sure the program will work with your MIDI equipment. There are only a few programs that specify certain instruments, the majority work with any MIDI equipment. At this stage check your instrument to see what sort of results are possible with a sequencer (i.e. the polyphony and multitimbral capabilities).
4 Having established that the program is suitable for your computer, MIDI interface and instrument, look at the specs for the sequencer. Check the number of tracks, the type of editing, GM/GS compatibility, MCI commands, the advanced features.
5 See if the sequencer has any upgrade path to more sophisticated versions with added features that you may require later.
6 If you want your files to be read by other software (notation programs or other sequencers) make sure the program will support the MIDI file format.
7 If printing is important check whether the program itself has staff notation which can be printed, or has a companion program that will print the files.
8 Check the price! There are many PC sequencer programs available – the prices vary considerably as do their features.

Using MIDI for remote control

When MIDI was introduced, it didn't take too long for people to realise that it could also be used for information transfer and remote control. Once you've linked your synthesiser up to MIDI then you can use that data link to access any feature that is available on it. This means that you can use MIDI in the same way as a computer network, allowing you to share information and facilities. So if your keyboard doesn't have a disk drive, you don't have to buy lots of expensive RAM cartridges, you can use the hard disk on your PC. This has the added bonus of giving you the sophisticated data manipulation facilities that are possible with the PC.

And it's not only sound modules that can be controlled in this way. Given the success of the MIDI standard, all sorts of other devices can be controlled, both in the studio and in live performance. Devices ranging from effects units (such as digital delays and reverbs) to audio mixing desks and video production equipment can be equipped with MIDI interfaces; you can even get MIDI controlled graphic equalisers. In fact the audio visual (AV) world is starting to use MIDI quite a lot in applications as diverse as MIDI controlled lighting rigs and laser shows or synchronising multiple slide projectors for corporate presentations and exhibitions. MIDI is used extensively in shows such as Jean Michele Jarre's mammoth extravaganzas, giving control over lighting, synthesiser set-ups as well as instrument control.

Patch librarians and editors

As mentioned in Chapter 1, as synthesisers became more complex, the designers started to store the parameters that described the various elements of a synthesiser voice in electronic form rather than having a knob for each parameter. These values such as the sound envelopes, waveform types and filter characteristics were then altered electronically using a small number of controls on the front panel. While this made the synthesisers more economic and allowed the instant recall of different voice programmes, it made the instrument far more difficult to program. It became much more difficult to visualise the patch, as only one parameter was available for editing at any one time, comparable to trying to paint your front hall through the letter box.

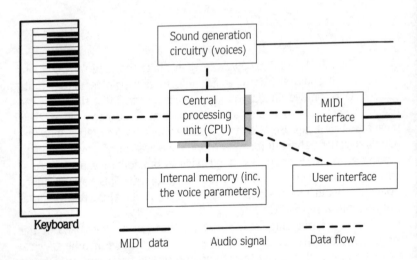

Figure 5.1 Schematic of the modern electronic synthesiser

With the advent of MIDI, manufacturers started to make the patch parameters accessible via MIDI system exclusive (SysEx) messages. This allowed two synthesisers of the same type to exchange voice (or patch) data. As computers became more common, this feature started to be used to store the voice parameters on disk and then to edit the voice on the computer. The main advantage that the computer has over the front panel of the synthesiser is that more information can be displayed on the VDU than on the small displays that tend to be common on synthesisers. There are some manufacturers such as Roland who produce remote programming panels for their keyboards and sound modules, but these are fairly rare and expensive. Certainly a computer – which you already own – and a piece of editing software is a more cost-effective solution.

So two types of program for manipulating the synthesiser voice data have appeared, the patch librarian and the patch editor. Quite often these two functions will be combined in a piece of software to give you total control over the sounds resident in your electronic instrument. Incidentally, the reason synthesiser voices are often called 'patches' harks back to the early days of computer synthesis. In the early modular instruments, the component sound modules had to be linked together with cables (or patch leads) to program the sounds. The connections to the modules would be accessible from a matrix of sockets called a patch panel. Thus the configuration required to get a particular voice or sound when the modules were connected together was called a patch. Obviously it was not a trivial or quick task to change the voice program on one of those instruments, a far cry from today when all you need to do is tap a button.

Patch librarian

A librarian will store and retrieve the synthesiser's voice data to and from the computer. On most synthesisers the voices are arranged in banks consisting of a number of individual patches. For instance on the Yamaha DX11 there are 32 memory locations that can store voices, these can be sent via MIDI individually or as a block of 32. These voice store locations are called RAM voices as they can be altered or replaced with new voices; most instruments also have ROM or pre-set voices that cannot be altered, but are set at the factory when the synthesiser is made and are thus called the manufacturer's pre-sets.

At its simplest, a librarian program will simply record any system exclusive message received on the MIDI In port and then replay it on demand from the MIDI OUT port. The program is relying on the fact that the synthesiser will always recognise and act on its own system exclusive messages. This won't work with some instruments as they require a more sophisticated protocol, perhaps expecting the receiver to confirm that it has received the data without error. More complex librarians will also allow you to change the order of the voices within a bank or swap voices between different banks, thus allowing you to get the best use out your synthesiser. Depending on the song you are working on, you can create a custom bank set-up for each piece. These librarians usually store not only the voice parameters but also such things as performance parameters, for instance, on some synthesisers you can set up 'performances' that combine voices to give you multi-layered or combined sounds. These can be stored by the librarian and then recalled on demand.

Obviously if the librarian is manipulating the voices within a bank, it needs to know the structure of the system exclusive for that particular instrument. This means that whereas the simple program could be used with almost any synthesiser, these more elaborate librarians are specific to a particular instrument, which is all right if you have only one or two instruments. If, on the other hand, you have a studio with a range of synthesisers, and furthermore you have to deal with hired instruments, you would need a librarian to keep track of the librarian programs.

To cover this situation there are programs that will handle a large number of different synthesisers, drum machines and effects units. These are sometimes called universal librarians or MIDI network managers, and will allow you to take 'snapshots' of your studio set-up so that you can easily restore the synthesiser voicings and effects parameters at some later date. So, for instance, you could store a client's set-up at the end of a recording session and then restore it at the start of their next session.

A good example of this type of software was Voyetra's Patch Master Plus program. This was available either as a stand-alone version or built into Voyetra's Sequencer Plus Gold sequencing package. Patch Master memorised system set-ups, each set-up can contain the details of up to 32 instruments. In this context, an instrument is any studio device that can use MIDI system exclusive messages to store its internal configuration.

The program supported over a hundred different MIDI modules with Voyetra adding new instruments as they were introduced. The voices in each sound bank could be swapped or copied within – or between – banks and each voice could be assigned a name of up to 20 letters to help you keep track of individual voices.

As well as the storage facilities, there was a comprehensive MIDI monitoring section which was helpful with troubleshooting your MIDI network or for storing and replaying system exclusive messages to synthesisers not otherwise supported.

Patch editor

If instead of simply cataloguing the sounds, you want to alter (or edit) the sound itself, you'll need to get a patch or voice editor. This type of software effectively copies a section of the synthesiser's memory into the computer (via MIDI) and allows you to manipulate it. When the data is copied back into the synthesiser (again via MIDI) any sound generation parameters that have been altered will be reflected in the sound. Patch editors come at many levels of complexity and price, from simple editors that display the patch parameters as numbers to high powered graphical editors. One recent trend has been towards universal or generic editors which, like the universal librarians, support more than one type of synthesiser. Some of these editors can be configured by the user to support any synthesiser and they all come with a set of pre-defined instruments.

What to look for

There are several things to look for in a voice editor and/or librarian. Apart from selecting one that matches your synthesiser you might consider whether the editor/librarian is compatible with your sequencer. This has the advantage of saving disk space on your computer since you will not have to keep multiple copies of the synthesiser voice data for use with each type of program. Another point to consider is whether you'll want to use the patch editor at the same time as the sequencer. If so then the editor will need to be able to run as a TSR (for DOS sequencers) so that you can pop it up over the sequencer.

Under Windows you only need to consider whether your MIDI device driver is multi-client or not. If it isn't then you should consider getting a pseudo MIDI device driver – such as the Lowrie-Woolf MIDI Master Plus – that can act as a kind of software MIDI merger. In general the programs with the 'friendliest' user interface will be more expensive, so unless you are expecting to do a lot of voice editing, a more basic program might be more appropriate.

Programming

If you do want to try your hand at programming a MIDI application, the easiest (and possibly most rewarding) way to start is to write a patch editor or librarian for your current keyboard. The system exclusive data format will either be described in the synthesiser's user manual or will be available from the manufacturer. The advantage of starting with this kind of program is that you don't need to worry about such things as the time relationship of the MIDI data, running status or the handling of multiple channels. It will also teach you a lot about your synthesiser and give a useful tool for making music.

If you can't find the data format from the above sources then it might be worth looking at The MIDI System Exclusive Book (see Appendix D). This book and all the MIDI specifications can be obtained from the International MIDI Association (IMA).

Sample editors

Whereas synthesisers predate cost-effective personal computer music systems, sampling keyboards and 'stand-alone' samplers have become practicable only fairly recently. In fact the technological advances that made samplers possible are a direct result of the personal computer revolution.

A sampler is effectively a digital recorder, it measures the level of an audio waveform at regular intervals and then stores each value as a number in the sampling device's memory. The sampler can then, at some later date, reconstitute the sound from these values by replaying them at the same rate as they were recorded.

The sampler can also alter the pitch of the sound by altering the rate at which the samples are replayed. The pitch will increase with the sampling rate, so doubling the replay rate will take the pitch up an octave, and halving it will take the pitch down an octave and so on.

Looping the loop

The amount of memory that is used to store a sample is directly proportional to the length of the sample multiplied by the sample rate. This can be quite wasteful for sounds that don't change much over time. An extreme example of this would be a simple organ sound, which, after an initial attack sound, settles down into a steady timbre or waveform.

Rather than waste sample memory on essentially redundant wave data, a technique called looping is used to repeat a small section of the sound repeatedly. The size of the repeated portion of sound can be as little as one cycle for simple waveforms, or quite long for a complex timbre such as a string section.

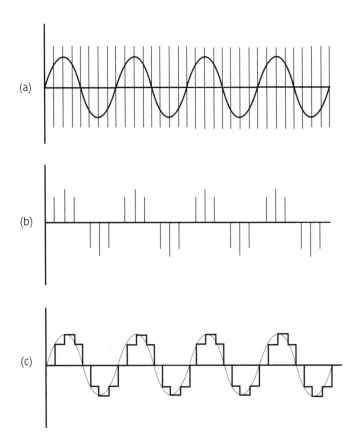

(a)

(b)

(c)

Figure 5.2 The elements of a sample
(a) The waveform to be sampled showing the sampling points
(b) What the computer sees. These are the actual voltages that are
read from the analogue to digital converter. These values are stored
into the computer memory.
(c) What we hear. The reconstituted waveform from the digital to
analogue converter, showing the original waveform (fine line). The
area between the curves is the quantisation error (sounds like noise).

As with the patch data, using MIDI we can read the data from
the sampler into the computer's internal memory for storage and editing purposes. The amount of data needed to describe a sample is usually much greater than that needed to describe a synthesiser voice, so

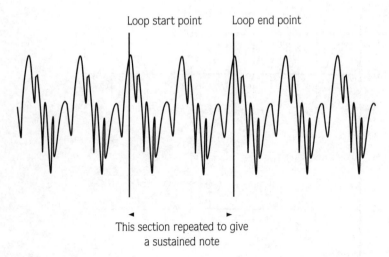

Figure 5.3 A portion of the sampled waveform can be repeated to give a sustained note

the transmission time is correspondingly greater. Once the sample data is in the computer you can alter the sound in various ways, such as trim the end points, set loop points, alter the harmonic structure of the sound and combine two different samples. Since one of the primary requirements of a sampler is to have large amounts of memory, the PC itself can be used as a sampler with the addition of a digital to analogue converter (DAC); this topic is covered in Chapter 6.

Another interesting thing that can be done with samplers and sample editing software is computer sample generation. This means that rather than the data being the recording of an acoustic sound, the sample is generated by the PC. Using this method you can perform additive synthesis which is where you define the frequency response of the sound and then get the computer to construct the corresponding waveform.

What to look for in a sample editor

The minimum requirement for a sample editor is that it should be possible to edit the start and end points of a sample and alter the loop points. The complexity of the looping will be defined by the sampler, but it should be possible to display the sample waveform around the loop points and help you select the best place for the loop. More sophisticated editors will also have options to alter the level of the sample, merge and mix samples, alter the frequency response of the sample and even create samples from scratch.

The sample dump standard

The data that makes up a sample is conceptually much easier to visualise than that of a synthesiser patch. This is because you are dealing with a direct representation of the actual sound rather than an arbitrary set of values that are used by an arcane piece of sound generation hardware. The other major difference between patch data and sample data is that the latter is a complete representation of the sound and as such is common between all samplers. Unlike synthesisers, there is no reason why you can't swap samples which were originally recorded on different makes of instruments.

The MIDI Manufacturers' Association (MMA) have recognised this common data format and have specified the MIDI sample dump standard (or SDS) which acts as a common language for samplers to transfer sample data. The standard covers only the lowest common denominator of the data, that is the sound data and basic loop definition, it obviously can't cater for all the different special features found on commercial samplers. Most modern samplers support the sample dump standard and certainly future instruments will be able to swap data this way.

Programming

Like the patch editor, the sample editor is a good place to start for DIY programmers, although interactive graphics are more important, and since there is more data to be transferred, larger memory may have to be used. Details of the sample dump standard are available from the International MIDI Association (IMA) and details of your sampler's system exclusive format will be found in either the instrument's user manual or from the manufacturer. Apart from editing sounds you could also experiment with different synthesis methods by using the computer to generate samples to be replayed by a sampler (see Chapter 6 for more details).

Synchronisation

So far in this chapter we've been talking about the control of the sound generation circuitry of an electronic instrument. It is important to remember that the computer is not necessarily going to be the only music playback device in your studio. And if there is more than one source of music then you are going to have to synchronise them. Synchronisation has two aspects, the first is to get the two music sources to start at the same time, the second is to keep the two independent systems in time with each other. It's just like playing in a band, you have to have some kind of count in so that you all start together and usually someone (perhaps a drummer or a conductor) will define the tempo and generally help the musicians to keep in time.

The history of synchronisation

Musicians have been trying to synchronise electronic instruments for as long as there have been suitable instruments to synchronise. In fact, before MIDI came on to the scene there was a burgeoning industry dedicated to making little black boxes that allowed drum machines and sequencers to play in time with each other. Some well known companies such as J L Cooper started out in this particular field.

The first method of synchronising different devices involved the first drum machines. These instruments divided a bar of music into a number of steps. Each step was selected sequentially by the drum machine's internal clock, and any of the percussive sounds could be triggered as the step was selected. The clock was an electronic pulse signal, each pulse being used to select the next step. So synchronising two drum machines was simply a matter of using the pulse or clock signal from one drum machine to drive the circuitry of the other. Unfortunately it wasn't as simple as this – the problem was that different manufacturers quite often used different clock resolutions, for instance Roland and Sequential used 24 pulses per quarter note (ppqn), Linn used 48 ppqn, Oberheim used 96 ppqn and the Fairlight CMI insisted on 384 ppqn.

This incompatibility was not the only problem; people soon realised how useful it would be to be able to make the drum machine play in time with a performance on tape. Unfortunately when it came to synchronising to a tape machine, the pulse method of synchronisation was not ideal since tape recorders will not record pulses particularly well and any phase inversion of the 'sync' signal (say in the mixing desk or tape pre-amp) compromised its usefulness. There were problems even when the signal was successfully recorded on to tape, the tape always had be started from the beginning of the sound since all the drum machine was doing was counting the pulses. This meant that if you wanted to do a five second over-dub at the end of a five minute song, you had to listen to the entire song before you could perform the over-dub.

Frequency shift keying

To solve the problem of recording the clock signal on tape frequency shift keying (FSK) was introduced. FSK encoded the pulse as an audio signal which made it easier to record the signal on tape and, since the clock was determined by a change in frequency, a phase inversion in the signal path wouldn't affect its accuracy. So it was now easier to get a reliable clock signal from the tape machine but there was still the problem of resolution incompatibilities between drum machines and the fact that the sequence or tape always had to be started at the beginning.

When MIDI came along it solved two major problems. First of all, it standardised a clock resolution for the synchronisation of separate devices and provided a method for starting anywhere within a sequence. It also added a method for selecting different sequences or

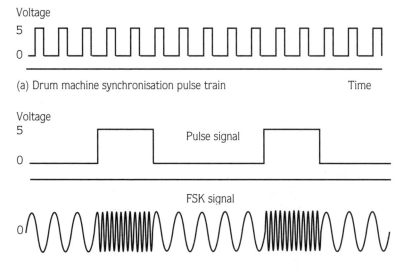

(a) Drum machine synchronisation pulse train   Time

(b) FSK synchronisation

Figure 5.4 Two different types of synchronisation – drum machine click and frequency shift keying (FSK)

songs on the drum machine. The MIDI clock resolution is 24 ppqn which may seem to be quite low by today's standards, but in fact most sequencers actually have higher resolutions than this – what they do is interpolate their own beats between the MIDI clock messages, using the MIDI beats to correct any timing inaccuracies than may have crept in since the previous MIDI clock message. Thus you could say that the sequencer is resynchronising 24 times per beat. The location of the starting bar within a sequence is performed by a song position pointer (SPP) message which defines the start in terms of MIDI beats. A MIDI beat is equal to six MIDI clocks and therefore is the same as a crotchet, or a quarter of a bar (i.e. in 4/4 time). So for instance to start at the beginning of the tenth bar in a 4/4 sequence, the SPP value would be 160, that is four (MIDI beats) times four (beats to the bar) times ten (bars).

While the MIDI synchronisation standard solved the problems of getting two drum machines to play together and paved the way for affordable multi-instrument sequencers, it did little to directly address the problem of synchronising to tape, since the MIDI signal cannot be recorded. Certainly, it was still possible to record start, stop and timing information on to tape as an FSK signal, but as sequencers become more complex, the constraint of always having to start the sequence from the start of the song became less tenable in a creative environment. To get around this problem several manufacturers (including Music Quest) developed variants of FSK that contained additional positional information. This meant that now the tape machine could be started anywhere in the song and the sequencer would locate the correct bar and then start playing in sync to the tape. In this situation the sequencer essentially becomes an extension of the tape machine giving up to 16 extra tracks, one per MIDI channel.

SMPTE/EBU timecode

Another solution to the tape sync problem that evolved was the use of SMPTE/EBU timecode. The video world had developed a method of editing video tapes that relied on recording a longitudinal timecode (or LTC) signal on the audio track. This timecode track uniquely defines each point on the tape in terms of hours, minutes, seconds and frames, so in video terms this means that each frame can be located. It is also possible to pin-point locations on the tape within a timecode frame down to 1/80 or 1/100 of a frame depending on the timecode reader. So timecode gives the positional information required for the sequencer to track the tape accurately, and, since music-to-video is a lucrative market for musicians, it wasn't long before time-code-to-MIDI converters appeared on the market. These converters take the timecode signal and produce MIDI sync signals that allow the sequencer to track the tape accurately. The tempo and start time must be programmed into the converter so that it can perform the calculations required to produce the MIDI clock messages.

Timecode versus FSK

There is a major difference between the way the tempo is encoded in FSK and timecode systems. With any FSK system, the tempo information is implicit in the signal, this is because the actual clock pulses are recorded on tape; if there is a tempo change then the timing of the MIDI clocks will change.

When a sequencer or a drum machine synchronises to an external MIDI clock, it has no way of knowing what the tempo is, it just moves on a step. So when an FSK track is recorded onto tape, the tempo is fixed from that point, since to change the tempo would require that the timing track be recorded again, and it would be almost impossible to get the start point correct. Timecode, on the other hand, has no tempo information encoded in it, the tempo is defined when the timecode is converted to MIDI. This means that the tempo can be altered at any time.

Having the tempo fixed in a short piece is probably not going to be a problem, however a longer piece with many sections might need to be changed as it evolves, with FSK timing the piece would need to be started from scratch each time there was an alteration to the tempo.

Timecode is not without its problems either. Since the timecode reader must have the tempo to do its conversion, we have the situation where the tempo is defined in a separate place from the rest of the sequence. Most readers have the ability to store a tempo map to allow for tempo changes in the sequence, but the storage of this information is another complication.

The ideal solution to this problem is to have the timecode reader built in to the sequencer, which is now possible due to the advent of MIDI interface cards such as the Music Quest and Voyetra offerings with integral readers. Another problem with external timecode readers is caused by inaccuracies in the timecode-to-MIDI calculations; ideally, all readers should produce the same MIDI signals given the same tempo and start information, unfortunately this is not always the case.

Arguably, the Yamaha C1 was the first fully functional sequencing system on the PC (or indeed on any computer) with its integral tape synchronisation to all timecode standards and multiple MIDI ports. With the Music Quest and Voyetra systems giving these facilities to standard PCs there is no reason why PC sequencing systems can't match the best of those found on other computers or dedicated sequencing systems.

MIDI timecode (MTC)

As the use of timecode became more ubiquitous in the music world, the MIDI Manufacturers' Association (MMA) and the Japan MIDI Standards Committee (JMSC) incorporated its features into the MIDI specification. This solved the problem of the tempo map conversion inaccuracies between different synchronisers since the tempo map could now be incorporated in the sequencer software. The advent of MTC also sounded the death knell of the MPU-401 as the *defacto* MIDI interface specification, since it can't synchronise its internal clock to the new timing protocol.

At its most basic level, MTC simply acts as a 'carrier' of the timecode output from a SMPTE/EBU synchroniser, allowing the MIDI software on the PC to keep track of the location on the master device – say a tape machine. Since the timecode converter now only has to do a protocol conversion between the analogue LTC signal and the MIDI based MTC, it can be a lot simpler to operate – and cheaper to make. The MTC protocol also incorporates 'cueing' messages that enable the MIDI timecode to control external devices – for instance slide projectors. This means that your MTC aware Audio Visual sequencer could download a list of events to the external device which would then control its own operation according to the incoming timecode. We don't know of any musical application that uses these facilities, but could see that they may be quite useful in certain situations.

MIDI Machine Control – MMC

Another commonly used addition to the MIDI specification is the MIDI Machine Control (or MMC) protocol which allows your PC – or rather its software – to control a tape transport. With this, your sequencer software can use a multitrack tape recorder as an extension to your PC based recording/sequencing system. The sequencer uses the MMC commands to tell the tape machine to play, record, stop and wind forwards or backwards, thus mirroring its own operation. This means that you can seamlessly integrate audio into your MIDI set-up, while still taking advantage of the benefits of the traditional multitrack tape format. The alternative to using tape is to record audio onto your PC's hard disk, a technique which is covered in Chapter 6.

While some multitrack recorders have MMC built-in, normally you will need to buy an MMC interface which will probably be specific to the particular type of tape recorder being controlled. For instance the Alesis ADAT eight track digital recorder has a number of off-the-shelf control boxes like the J L Cooper Datasync 2 and the Steinberg ACI that let you slave this machine to any sequencer that implements MMC. Both these devices allow your sequencer software to control the tape transport which – in turn – provides a synchronisation signal using MIDI timecode (MTC) so that the sequencer will stay in step with any slight speed variations of the tape transport. This sounds an odd kind of 'push-me/pull-you' arrangement, but can prove to be a very effective and robust form of integrated tape/MIDI recording system which can be achieved at a reasonable cost.

Practical situations

There are probably going to be two basic situations where you will want to synchronise different devices. The first is where you want to synchronise two MIDI devices such as a drum machine and a computer, and the second is where you want to synchronise a MIDI device to a non-MIDI device such as a tape recorder. In both these cases one machine will be the sync master and all the devices will be slaves, that is derive their timing from the master device.

Synchronising two MIDI devices

In the first case the master will probably be a PC-based sequencer and the slave will be one or more drum machines. The only thing you need to be careful of here is that the sequencer is sending MIDI real-time messages. Some sequencers allow you to switch off real-time or timing messages to reduce the density of the MIDI data in order to minimise any MIDI delays or 'choke' problems. MIDI choke is where there is too much information to be sent down the MIDI cable at a particular point in time, causing some of the data to be delayed, rather like a digital traffic jam.

Synchronising MIDI to tape

The second case is probably the most common synchronisation situation in the music studio. The tape machine is almost always the sync master in this case, as it is rather expensive to synchronise the tape transport. The first thing that needs to be done here is to record the synchronisation signal onto one of the tracks, this is called 'striping'. The signal is usually recorded onto an edge track to reduce the possibility of 'crosstalk', since it has only one adjacent track. The major issue here is crosstalk between the synchronisation track and the adjacent audio track. On narrow tape formats, the sync signal may leak into the adjacent channel on playback, giving a high pitched warble. If this is a problem then you may have to leave an empty track between the sync track and the rest of the audio tracks, which means that you lose two tracks rather than just the one dedicated to the sync code. The problem can be reduced by recording the sync track at as low a level as you can get away with, however in this case you would have to be careful what you record on the adjacent track: bass or drums could disrupt the sync signal with disastrous results.

Apart from crosstalk, the other most common form of synchronisation problem is due to what are known as drop-outs. A drop-out is a momentary loss of signal (in this case the sync signal) usually due to a tape imperfection. This sort of problem can be reduced by using high quality mastering tape such as Ampex 456 or similar. Any decent synchroniser will compensate for this type of error by 'fly-wheeling'. This means that the sync reader will realise that the sync signal has disappeared and continue to produce a synchronisation signal based on its own internal time-base. The longer the period of the signal loss, the more likely this calculated signal will drift with respect to the tape machine. A synchroniser will normally fly-wheel for one or two seconds before giving up the ghost, which is quite adequate to cover most drop-outs.

SMPTE/EBU timecode has a slight edge over smart FSK here, since with FSK, the tempo is implicitly encoded onto the tape. So, if a drop-out occurs on a tempo change, the FSK reader will not realise this until the sync signal returns, so a momentary timing error will occur. SMPTE/EBU on the other hand will only cause this kind of error if the tape transport radically changes speed, which would lead to other problems such as pitch changes.

What to look for

If you are synchronising your PC you have two choices. The first is to buy an interface with built-in sync facilities and the second is to buy an external device that will convert the synchronisation signal on tape into MIDI timing information. The original MPU-401 interface has a simple FSK interface built into it, which is fine for occasional use, and is supported by most PC DOS software, but is not suitable for any sort of serious use. This means that you must have a positional synchronisation scheme, such as 'smart' FSK or SMPTE/EBU time code. Music Quest interfaces were one of the first to support positional synchronisation with their smart FSK and SMPTE interfaces, though they initially had very little software available to support these features. The introduction of the Voyetra V24s card and the Yamaha C1 provided more choice, both in terms of interface cards and software available. The integration of the timecode reader/writer is undoubtedly the most desirable configuration, since all the information to do with tempo can then be stored with your other sequence data.

This leaves us with external synchronisation boxes – the choice of which will depend largely on your budget. The device will need to be able to read and write the synchronisation signal from/to the tape machine, set the start timecode (SMPTE/EBU only) and have the ability to 'fly-wheel' to recover from tape dropouts. Since the introduction of MTC, there is now no need to have external tempo map stored in the synchroniser – the sequencer can handle this – which simplifies the entire synchronisation process considerably. If you do have to use MIDI SPP and clock pulses, your synchroniser will need to be able to store a tempo map and dump its internal configuration via MIDI system exclusive messages (or use some other method for storing this information) and – for SMPTE/EBU timecode readers – then be able to set up time offsets. Have a look at the product range of J L Cooper's and XRI to get a feel for what's available in the world of synchronisers.

Synchroniser purchase checklist

1 Make sure you have a spare track on your project tape to record a timecode signal. You really need to be able to turn off noise reduction – say Dolby – for reliable operation.

2 Will your sequencer let you use MIDI Time Code? If not consider upgrading to a different package.

3 Does your sequencer support MIDI machine control? If it does then see if you can get a synchroniser for your tape machine that supports this protocol.

4 If you have only one MIDI input port, make sure that the synchroniser can merge (i.e. mix) the MIDI output from your controller with the MTC signal. If it can't, you may need to purchase an extra MIDI merge device.

5 Decide whether you need an external synchroniser or a MIDI interface with timecode facilities.

6 Check the price! There are many synchronisers available on the market – the prices vary considerably as do their features.

The PC as a sound source

Unlike other home computers (e.g. Macintosh, Commodore, Amiga), the IBM PC has no 'built-in' hardware for producing sound, other than a simple speaker. Both Macintosh and Amiga computers have dedicated sound chips which are programmable and can be very flexible in their capabilities (depending on the model). However the PC requires additional hardware to achieve real musical results. This lack of built-in audio hardware is a two-edged sword. In a way it is a problem because it means there is no 'standard' way of making a noise on the PC – apart from a few basic beeps using the built-in speaker. On the other hand the PC expansion bus means that you can add a sophisticated sound generator that can be changed as the technology improves without having to scrap the computer – which is what you would need to do if the sound generator was integral to the computer.

Sound generation on the PC is not entirely without standards though. The introduction of multimedia elements into Windows 3.1 made it possible to define an overall multimedia standard for the PC which encompassed audio – amongst other things. The Multimedia PC sound standard (or MPC) defines the basic audio capabilities expected to be available in the Windows environment and incorporates digital audio, CD audio and MIDI. This standard is discussed in greater detail in the next chapter.

Different approaches to PC sound

There are two basic approaches to producing high quality sound with the PC: you can install a music synthesiser into it, or you can get it to play back the raw audio data from the hard disk.

Internal synthesiser

The former method has a lot in common with using the PC to control external MIDI devices (as covered in Chapter 5). Integrating a synthesiser into the PC does give a number of advantages over an external device in that the computer can have more complete control over the sound generating hardware, without the speed limitations of the MIDI protocol. This last point can be quite important if you need to transfer large amounts of data to the synthesiser – for instance when programming a sound generator that uses audio samples. The quality of the sound produced is totally independent of the power or capabilities of the PC, being determined entirely by the quality of the additional hardware. This has resonances with the 'intelligent' MIDI interface, essentially off-loading the task from the PC's processor to a dedicated piece of hardware.

Digital audio approach

The alternative to using a synthesiser card is to play back digital audio – essentially turning the PC into a glorified tape recorder. This process is very similar to the sampler technology described in the previous chapter except that the audio data will usually be read from hard disk, thus avoiding the storage limitations of a RAM-based sampler.

Technically, the digital audio replay approach is simpler than an internal synthesiser, but it does put a lot more strain on the PC's processor. This is because the PC now has to read the data off the hard disk and transfer it to the digital-to-analogue converters (DACs) on a soundcard. For CD quality this means that the PC has to read four eight-bit samples (i.e. stereo 16 bit) 44,100 times a second and send them to the DAC. Failure to do this will cause clicks or 'stutter' effects on the audio output. While this process still has a hardware component – i.e. the soundcard's DAC – this is a lot simpler and more 'general purpose' than a synthesiser card.

However, despite these problems, the digital audio approach to PC sound is undoubtedly the 'wave of the future' since it is a lot more adaptable than the hardware approach. However it will take processors an order of magnitude more powerful than those currently available to make best use of the facilities that become available when you start handling the audio directly.

Software synthesis

One interesting recent development is that of 'software' synthesisers. This is where the PC's processor generates the sounds from scratch, using sound synthesis algorithms to mimic the function of a hardware sound module. The results are then sent to the soundcard's DAC to be converted into an audio signal. The big advantage of this approach is that you can change the type of synthesis by simply loading new software, which is a lot easier than swapping synthesiser cards. The software is pretty basic at the moment but as faster processors become available both the quality and the diversity of algorithms should improve.

The PC loudspeaker

The PC speaker is the most basic of sound generation devices on the PC. Its sole advantage is that every PC has one. Although the basic speaker circuitry will be more or less compatible, there will be variations from machine to machine which can affect the quality of the output. At its most basic level the speaker can be controlled from a program to produce a pitch using a simple square waveform. It is thus possible to play melody lines of simple tunes. Some basic music software does use the speaker to play back melody lines. In particular, DOS-based educational software, concerned with early learning skills of rhythm and pitch, use the PC speaker to interact with the student. However, it is quite difficult to get the speaker to play polyphonically, and the results are pretty poor. This means that any chords must either be ignored, or the individual notes of the chord separated out and played as an arpeggio. The restrictions have encouraged the use of additional hardware to bring sound to the PC.

Under Windows it is possible to use the PC speaker as a more sophisticated digital audio output device, using either Microsoft's unsupported speaker device driver or various public domain drivers. The results are very variable depending on how the speaker hardware is configured on a particular PC, and may not work at all on certain systems. The device driver treats the speaker as a one-bit digital to analogue converter (DAC) and uses pulse width modulation to create a suitable audio power spectrum for the sound being reproduced. The problems with this method are twofold; since there is no output filtering on the speaker output, the audio is very harsh – and relies on the ear to 'join' the dots. Secondly the process of converting the digital audio data into an analogue signal is very processor intensive and can have a detrimental effect on the operation of any other software that happens to be running on the PC.

Synthesiser cards

The use of additional hardware actually fits in quite well with the basic design concept of the PC, where the computer provides the brain and any special functions are provided by expansion cards. Consider what would have happened if IBM had added sound generation to the original PC design in 1981 – music hardware has developed by such a great extent that any internal sound circuitry would now be laughably out of date.

Currently the most cost-effective way to make the computer produce high quality sound directly is to put a synthesiser inside the machine on an expansion card. Software then addresses the card directly to program and play back sound. The original cards were designed to add sounds to computer-based games software and, as there were no generally accepted standards, the early cards were a bit of a mixed bag with regard to compatibility and software support. In recent years the *de facto* standard for soundcards has been based on either the Roland MPU-401 (for MIDI cards) or the Creative Labs SoundBlaster range (for digital audio replay).

IBM Music Feature card

One of the first synthesiser cards to appear that incorporated MIDI was the IBM Music Feature. The card, which was full length and had MIDI connections and stereo output, was introduced into the USA in 1987 as a joint venture between IBM and Yamaha. The resulting card used the electronics from one of Yamaha's existing FM synthesiser modules (the FB-01), coupled with a passive MIDI interface. The Music Feature had a polyphony of eight notes, with eight instruments selectable at any one time from a list of 240. The card unfortunately suffered from the fact that nearly all the available PC-based music software was using the already established MPU-type MIDI interface from Roland and consequently it would only run dedicated software.

Only a few software manufacturers (Jim Miller's Personal Composer being one) gave the option within the software of talking to the IBM Music Feature as well as the MPU interface. The card was also not taken on by IBM UK and thus has been hard to find in the UK.

Roland LAPC-1 card

Roland released a similar card in 1989 – the LAPC-1. This time the MIDI interface was the standard MPU type, and the sound generation was a super-set of Roland's existing MT-32 sound module. The fact that the interface was based on the MPU-401 meant that all existing music software (regardless of manufacturer) which used the MPU protocol would run with the card. Thus on the day it was released there was a complete and established range of software already available.

The synthesiser part of the card used Roland's popular Linear Arithmatic Synthesis technique, where pre-set samples of transients are combined with synthesised sound to produce a realistic copy of existing sounds. The card offered the user 128 different sounds to choose from plus a full drum kit, a set of percussion and several sound effects. These can be used through eight MIDI channels plus an additional channel for the drums, percussion and sound effects and can be panned between the left and right outputs. The total polyphony of the device is 32.

When installed in the PC the card acts and responds exactly the same as an MPU type interface attached by a MIDI lead to a Roland MT32 or CM32L sound module. In this way Roland introduced no new standards but merely a new design and a more practical approach to the challenge of PC sound.

The LAPC card is interesting in a number of ways since it pointed the way for a number of later developments. Roland's GS sound set and multitimbral capabilities can be traced back to the success of the LAPC/MT-32 range of synthesisers. You could even argue that the LAPC concept trail-blazed the way for the later introduction of the General MIDI standard.

Another standard that can be traced back to the Roland synthesiser is the Windows MPC Extended sound set. The LAPC card with its high quality audio output and relatively high degree of multitimbrally meant that the PC could be used as a stand-alone music workstation, simply requiring the addition of a relatively simple external MIDI keyboard to make it a self-contained music making system.

SoundBlaster card

While the LAPC-1 and its successors like the SCC-1 (Roland Sound Canvas) have been developed from music industry products and technology, other soundcards currently available have been developed primarily for use with games software. The most common – and thus the generally accepted standard – is the SoundBlaster card from Creative Labs. Unlike the soundcards previously discussed, the SoundBlaster combines a number of functions, the two primary audio functions are the replay of digital audio and the built-in synthesiser. The original games card standard was based on the Ad Lib Card which used FM technology to give 11 instruments simultaneously available (i.e. 11 note polyphony).

Creative Labs took the AdLib standard, enhanced it and added the ability to replay digital audio files. The early SoundBlaster cards offered 24 voices available to the user (the first 11 of these Ad Lib compatible). The major advance was the addition of a sample replay section, complete with an input which allowed the recording of real sounds. The sampling capability was pretty basic, but using a sample rate of 5 kHz, a recognisable sample is retained without eating into too much memory, (13 seconds for 64K without compression). The card had a wide range of games software that supported it – which more than anything else contributed to its success. It also had a rather basic MIDI interface (not MPU compatible) which made it suitable to use with external musical instruments, though software support was fairly patchy. When Windows 3.1 was introduced, SoundBlaster support was included (along with MPU-401) further enhancing its acceptance as a 'standard'.

With the introduction of 16 bit sample replay at CD sampling resolutions and wave-table synthesis, the SoundBlaster – and its many clones – can be considered for use in a music production system. The facilities provided by the SoundBlaster type of MPC soundcard make it ideal for an integrated MIDI + audio workstation, with the bulk of the music being produced using the MIDI features and using the digital audio section to record vocal lines or a featured solo instrument. The configuration and uses of this type of soundcard are considered in more detail in Chapter 7.

Sampling

The technical advances that made PCs possible have also brought the price of memory low enough to make sound samplers practicable. Since a sampler is essentially an analogue to digital converter (ADC) with lots of memory, and the PC already has the memory, all we need to add to the PC is the conversion circuitry to get us a sampler. So with additional hardware the PC can be used to capture real sounds, and play them back.

To recap, the idea behind sampling is that a real sound is recorded either by a microphone or directly from a sound source, and is converted to a digital signal, which can be stored in memory. On playback the signal is re-converted back to an analogue signal which can be amplified, effectively reconstituting the original sound. The technique is called sampling because the process involves taking snapshots or samples of the audio signal and assigning them a binary number corresponding to the height of the waveform at that time. The more samples taken per second, the more numbers, and the more accurate the conversion of the real sound. Always associated with any sampling device will be a sample rate, that is how many times per second a reading is taken. For digital audio (used for CD preparation) the rate is 44.1 kHz, thus a reading of the analogue signal is taken 44,100 times each second. The other specification always made is how accurate (or precise) the digital number that describes an individual sample is. Again for digital audio in both the consumer and professional music industry the standard is 16 bit samples except for some specialised applications – mainly for classical recordings – where 20, 22 or even 24 bit sampling may be used.

There are actually two ways for a PC to use samples, the simplest method is that implemented by MPC soundcards and is simply a matter of storing the sampled sound on hard disk and then replaying on demand. The stored data can be manipulated by a sample editor which can allow the user to cut and paste sections of the sound, but otherwise the sound is simply read off the hard disk and squirted out of the digital to analogue converters on the soundcard. For this kind of sampling it is impracticable to try to hold the sampled sound in the computer memory. As an example, a 16 bit stereo sample recorded at a rate of 44.1kHz, would require approximately 100 kilobytes of memory for each second – or over 10 megabytes for a minute of sound.

The alternative is to integrate a 'musical instrument' sampler onto a PC expansion card. Samplers were discussed in the Chapter 5, and the only major difference between a PC-based sampler and a stand-alone unit is that the former doesn't have any recording capability unless it is integrated with a more general purpose digital audio card – say an MPC soundcard. These 'sampler on a card' products are often referred to as RAM-based wave-table synthesisers, to differentiate them from sample-based synthesisers (also referred to as wave-table synthesisers) that store their samples in ROM. Like their stand-alone brethren, RAM-based soundcards incorporate the electronics to loop and alter the pitch of the samples and replay the audio data polyphonically. The cards don't use the PC's RAM, but have varying amounts of RAM installed on the expansion card, which can be loaded from data files stored on the PC's hard disk. Cards range in capability from the modestly equipped Gravis UltraSound (1 megabyte of RAM, stereo) to the fully professional SampleCell II from Digidesign which can take up to 32 megabytes of RAM and has eight individual audio outputs.

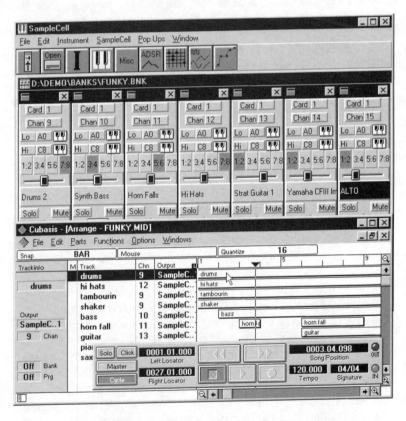

Figure 6.1 The combination of a sampling card and a MIDI sequencer gives a very powerful and adaptable music-making system

The RAM based wave-table sampler cards are usually only supported by Windows music applications, to which they appear as MIDI devices. The cards invariably come with support software that lets you to create your own sample banks based on the Windows – or RIFF – format sample files (i.e. WAV files). Pre-programmed banks are also becoming commercially available for the more popular cards. The advent of these cards has been a real boon to the PC based musician since it allows a much larger tonal palette than can be achieved using conventional soundcards. The latter tend to have sound sets based on the General MIDI standard – which by definition are all meant to sound the same.

MOD files and music trackers

Music modules – or MOD – files originated on the Commodore Amiga range of computers and were designed to take advantage of the sample replay hardware while minimising the amount of processor power and memory required. The basic idea is to store short music samples in the computer's memory and then alter the playback sample rate to get the 'pitched' notes of the music. To do this, MOD files contain both sample data and the music data, i.e. when to play each sample and at what pitch. MOD files usually contain a relatively small number of samples – say 15 or 31 – which are played back in 4, 8 or even 16 or 32 tracks if you have a Gravis Ultrasound card. The MOD concept is an interesting approach to getting the most out of a fairly limited set-up, but has been made rather redundant by advances in computer technology.

The original Amiga format allowed only up to four tracks of music data, but the specification has been tweaked by software designers as computer technology has advanced. As far as the authors are aware, the only available editing packages for creating MOD files – referred to as 'trackers' – run only under DOS. There are MOD file players that run under Windows, but these do not allow you to modify existing – or create new – MOD files. Since trackers run only under DOS they tend to be specific to particular soundcards – with the Creative Labs' SoundBlaster and the Gravis UltraSound cards being most widely supported.

All the PC MOD file tracker software known to us uses a list based editor interface, which is a good indication of the ancestry of the software. While the results can be quite effective, the process of creating a MOD file appears to be a fairly non-intuitive process. The only interest that a PC-based composer might have in this format is that some computer and console based games creators use the MOD files as their 'native' music soundtrack format. There are utilities for converting MOD files into MIDI files available but the results can be variable.

Most tracker software is available as shareware and tends to be used by computer enthusiasts rather than musicians or composers due – in the main – to the 'unfriendly' user interface mentioned above. As the MOD file is a public 'standard', there tend to be different flavours, often depending on the capabilities of the soundcard attached to the system, so be prepared for compatibility problems if you decide to use this format. Most of the MOD file editing and replay packages – along with many data files – are available for download from on-line services such as CIX or Compuserve. MOD support and data files also often appear on Public Domain and Shareware compilation CD's – like the Makin Musik disk from CD Exchange.

Hard disk recording

Whilst computer-based samplers could be considered to be a form of recording, the time durations are relatively short compared to the length of the piece of music. As the price of hard disk drive has reduced it has become economical actually to record long periods of sound in the same manner as a traditional tape recorder – using the hard disk as the recording medium. This gives the opportunity to per-form the kind of tricks that we can do with synthesiser patches and sampled notes on a complete recording. This kind of system is often referred to as a non-linear editing system since – unlike tape – you can replay any portion of the audio without having to first wind the tape to the appropriate data. This ability is due to the 'random access' nature of the PC's hard disk and is a very powerful weapon in the music maker's arsenal.

Non destructive editing

One of the fundamental techniques of non-linear audio systems is called non-destructive editing. This means that once the audio has been recorded on the hard disk, it is never altered. The replay and editing processes use data structures that 'point' to sections (or seg-ments) of the audio file – usually an offset from the start, and the length of the particular audio segment. This has two major benefits:

the first is that the audio data doesn't have to be directly manipulated, speeding up the editing process considerably. The second is that performing an edit never causes audio data to be 'lost' so you can always get back to your original recorded sound, and furthermore edits do not require any more disk space than the original recording.

To illustrate the significance of this technique, consider copying an audio track from one section of a song to another. If we had to physically move the data from one part of the disk to another – assuming a fairly conservative transfer rate of 1.2 Mbytes per second – it would take nine seconds to move a minute of audio data and twice this for a stereo sample. With a non-destructive editor the copying process takes virtually no time at all – as all that is happening is that a new data-structure is created. To control the overall playback of the audio segments that make up a complete song, these pointers are stored in a data table or event list usually referred to as an EDL (edit decision list) – a term borrowed from the video world.

MPC issues

While a hard disk recording system can be achieved using a standard MPC Windows soundcard, these are not ideal for this purpose as they are really designed for replaying short 'sound bytes' as either fairly low resolution speech or sound effects. MPC soundcards can be used effectively in hybrid MIDI/digital audio applications – but they usually do not perform well enough to cope with the real-time requirements demanded of a non-linear editing system. Also a lot of popular soundcards rule themselves out of the hard disk recording scene by lacking the ability to record and play back audio simultaneously. The lack of this feature means that it is impossible to over-dub 'in sync' with material already recorded on disk. Some software packages can get around this problem by allowing you to install multiple soundcards, which also has the advantage of giving more individual outputs.

Another problem with MPC-based systems is the inability to synchronise effectively with external devices like tape machines. The problem is that the mechanical transport of a tape recorder will fluctuate in the short term and possibly drift over the long term. The normal method of compensating for these small variations is to subtly vary the replay sample rate to track (or chase) the tape. Unfortunately the MPC control interface provides no fine control over the soundcard's sample rate, so the replay of the samples will gradually get out of step with the audio or video tape machine it is trying to chase. In general an MPC based non-linear editor will have inferior performance to a dedicated system – both in terms of the performance and facilities provided.

Hybrid systems

One of the most powerful ways of using a MPC-equipped PC is to combine the MIDI and audio facilities to produce a hybrid system that gives you the best of both worlds. With software like Cubasis Audio from Steinberg you can use MIDI to provide the backing track and then add a vocal or guitar part using the digital audio part. You can do this with virtually any soundcard since you can record only one audio track at any point in the song. This process relies on the MIDI and audio tracks remaining in synchronisation during playback, which is no problem as long as you play back the music only on the system on which it was recorded.

This is because the speed of the digital audio playback is determined by the speed of the crystal on the soundcard, which can vary from card to card. A variation of 0.5% will mean that after a couple of minutes the audio would be over a second out of sync (i.e. two beats at 120 BPM). The same thing can happen if you change your soundcard – say to upgrade it. You can reduce the problem by chopping up your audio into smaller chunks, which means that your audio is being resynchronised more often, but this only reduces the problem, it doesn't eliminate it. This problem is due to the fact the MIDI and audio are 'implicitly' synchronised which means that, once they start, they carry one without regard to anything else. On professional systems (see below), the audio and MIDI are 'explicitly' synchronised to a common timebase (say SMPTE timecode) which means that the replay software is constantly making tiny changes to the playback speed to ensure they remain 'in sync'.

Dedicated systems

There are two approaches to implementing an effective 'dedicated' hard disk recorder on the PC, the simplest is to record the audio onto the PC's hard disk and use the PC processor to perform all the signal processing tasks. There are a number of software packages that enable you to do this, the most popular being Software Audio Workshop (SAW) which supports a number of popular soundcards. The SAW application maximises the performance of the PC by being programmed in assembler language and by directly accessing the soundcard's audio hardware rather than using the Windows software interface. The performance of the system will be determined by the power of the PC running it, so for instance to replay 16 virtual tracks you need a Pentium 90 with 16 Mbyte of RAM. You need at least a 386DX40 PC to use the software at all. Running other applications simultaneously – say a sequencer – will adversely affect the performance of the SAW system, since you are reducing the computing resource available to the non-linear editor. Performance will also depend on the hard disks you have installed in your PC and the speed of the internal bus.

Hardware based systems

The alternative to the SAW approach is to install additional hardware to handle the digital audio and thus relegate the PC to becoming a graphical user interface. There are a number of systems that take this approach; they incorporate a digital signal processor (DSP) to handle the audio and separate hard disks to store that data. This separation of the digital audio disk storage from the PC's internal 'program' disks avoids the ISA bus 'bottleneck' allowing more tracks to be replayed and recorded. The DSP also speeds things up by performing all the audio processing – a task to which it is ideally suited, unlike the PC's processor. The advantage of this extra processing power is that the system can do more, do it faster, and achieve higher quality than either of the previous approaches. The downside of this approach is that the system will cost somewhat more since there is more duplication of resources such as hard disks and processing.

There are other advantages to adding in hardware to help with the task of recording audio onto the PC's hard disk. One of these is to allow extra audio inputs. For instance the Session-8 system from Digidesign (Figure 6.2) and the AudioPrisma from Spectral give you eight individual inputs and outputs. While you could get the same number of physical connections by installing four MPC compatible soundcards, this would be a very cumbersome arrangement. These systems also usually implement effective synchronisation and digital I/O (either S/PDIF or AES/EBU) so you can transfer the final result to digital audio tape (DAT) in the digital domain to eliminate further quality degradation due to the digital to analogue conversion process.

Although there are still some DOS-based systems around, in the main, most of these dedicated non-linear editing systems are based

Figure 6.2 DSP enhanced systems like Digidesign's Session-8 are powerful enough to replace traditional multitrack tape recorders

around Windows applications. The software usually incorporates an audio editor that lets you rearrange the audio data on disk (or rather the EDL 'pointers'). This supporting software will allow for editing sections both in terms of the cut and paste of sections – allowing you to rearrange the order in which the audio segments are replayed – and duplication of segments.

The audio waveform can usually be displayed on screen, with zoom in functions which allow any clicks and problems in the audio to be removed, zooming out to enable sections of waveform to be cut and copied. Sections can be reversed, repeated, played at different speeds, and the playback order of the samples can be rearranged. Playback of sections of music or short sound effects can be 'fired off' at specific times according to the play list, and complete automatic control is achieved when the computer is made to read and respond to an external time-code source.

The result is similar to our MIDI sequencer, but instead of the computer controlling external synthesisers that in turn create the noise, the computer itself replays pre-recorded sounds from hard disk.

Some drawbacks of hard disk systems

While the hard disk recorder is a very powerful tool for recording and manipulating audio, you do need to be aware of a couple of pitfalls. The first the necessity to have the means of backing up the audio data when the hard disk becomes full. By the very nature of a hard disk its capacity is limited and thus will fill up eventually and – unless you're going to throw away the material at the end of each editing session – you'll need some off-line storage. Professional systems do usually provide a means to backup to DAT via a digital interface, but low cost systems will need to have a tape drive, removable hard disk or similar.

The other consideration is the size and type of hard disk you need to use. Audio files are comparatively large files – over 5 megabytes per track minute of audio – and thus require a large amount of disk space.

For instance a 500 megabyte hard disk will store just under 50 minutes of audio, but if you are using it on an eight-track system, total running time decreases to just over six minutes. This is a bit of an over simplification since a hard disk system uses its storage resources more efficently than a tape based system, but the general principle holds. You also need to make sure that the hard disk is fast enough to sustain the data transfer rates required during playback and that the drive won't re-calibrate itself in the middle of playback. There are hard disk drives designed specifically for this kind of application – like the Micropolis AV range – which address these problems.

What to look for in a hard disk recorder

The best hard disk recorder for a particular situation will depend on the production environment and the intended final result. For instance the musician who works mainly with MIDI instruments but requires some recording capability would be best served by an integrated sequencing/audio package like Cubase Audio. Alternatively, if CD mastering or video dubbing facilities were required an entirely different system would be needed.

There are two important aspects that you must consider when deciding on which hard disk recording system you need. The most obvious is that the system must have the facilities you need to accomplish the required tasks. The second aspect is that the system should perform these tasks in a reasonable amount of time and at a suitable audio quality. It is pointless having a hard disk editing system that – regardless of its capabilities – can't perform them in a reasonable time scale or to the required audio quality. Thus if you are working in a situation that requires a high 'throughput' of projects, you will need a faster system than if you are just using the system for the occasional project.

In general the systems that perform the best are those that incorporate an independent DSP and disk sub-system for the digital audio. It is not surprising that these are also the most expensive – for reasons outlined above. These systems are designed to be used in professional audio production environments and therefore must be fast enough for the engineers to use them day in and day out.

On the other hand, a semi-professional musician might be content with a system that takes a few minutes to do a task that on a more expensive system would take seconds, because time is not as pressing and the musicality is more important than throughput.

MIDI/audio system

This application of digital audio is the logical extension of MIDI sequencing. There are two ways of implementing this kind of system; the fully integrated MIDI/audio application and running two applications (one audio based, the other MIDI based) concurrently on the same PC.

The former has advantages in that the user interface is identical regards of whether MIDI or audio is being edited. The disadvantage of the integrated approach is that your choice of audio hardware is considerably more limited, usually to MPC audio and one other system (if you are lucky).

For instance Cubase Audio on the PC supports only MPC audio and the Yamaha CBX-D5 hard disk recording hardware. Using two separate applications does give minor problems with swapping between two applications, but the programs can be more focused on their primary purpose – rather than trying to do everything.

Track laying

Track laying is a term coined by the professional audio and video industries to describe the process of multitrack recording. As this might involve recording a number of tracks – say an entire rhythm or brass section – you need to have a system with multiple inputs like the Digidesign Session-8 or the Spectral AudioPrisma. Both these systems allow you essentially to replace a multitrack tape recorder with a hard disk system. Although some of the MPC systems do support multiple outputs using multiple soundcards, Windows will not allow more than one track to be recorded at one time. A slight variation on this theme is the development of a number of 'hybrid' tape/hard disk systems like the Digidesign ADAT interface for the Session-8 which give the advantages of both media formats along with a convenient way to back-up the hard disk data.

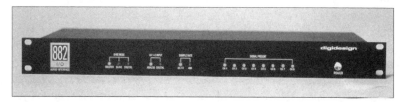

Figure 6.3 Using an external audio interface – like this Digidesign unit – will always give better audio quality

CD mastering

Once the music has been mixed – usually to DAT – you almost invariably need to compile the material into the correct order ready for creating the final product – i.e. cassette or CD production master. Unlike traditional analogue master formats, you can't manually edit a DAT with a razor blade and splicing tape. The normal technique is to copy the contents of the DAT back onto the hard disk system and then compile the audio segments into the final running order. Since the editing process is so simple, it is possible to perform sophisticated edits that would not have been contemplated on an analogue master, for fear of damaging the master tape. This means that an individual track can be mixed in sections and then 'glued' back together using the non-linear editor.

The best system currently on the market for this kind of work is the SADiE hard disk editor from Studio Audio & Video Limited. Other systems that can be used for this task effectively are SAW and Samplitude, with the proviso that the PC needs a digital interface so that the audio can be transferred as digital information. This is not so important for cassette mastering, but the conversion artefacts caused by multiple copying of the audio between your mastering medium and the hard disk will gradually degrade the quality, thus removing one of the advantages of recording digitally.

Video/audio and radio post-production

This application (sometimes called 'dubbing') requires that the various types of audio material – speech, sound effects and music – are mixed together to produce a soundtrack. Although not mandatory, it is very useful if these elements can be kept separate up to the final mix. To do this the system needs at least ten tracks, as well as the ability to cross-fade and otherwise manipulate the tracks in various ways. Owing to the nature of the editing process, the system needs to be very responsive since any delays will multiply because of the number of operations than need to be performed. The systems that come closest to fulfilling this task are the Spectral AudioEngine and AudioPrisma (more than ten tracks), the SADiE and Soundscape (very fast editing).

Future development

Since the first edition of this book the digital audio side of PC audio has expanded at a tremendous rate, from a few expensive and not very 'user friendly' systems to a point where they are superseding traditional dedicated digital audio workstations (DAW). This is in the main, due to the tremendous decrease in the price per megabyte of hard disk storage, but the recognition of the power of non-linear editing over traditional techniques is also an important factor.

You could draw a parallel between the audio world and the Desk Top Publishing (DTP) revolution of the late 1980's. The adoption of Windows as the world's most popular operating environment has ensured that the PC has been at the forefront of this technical revolution, and will probably mean that it will stay a front runner in the field of digital audio technology.

It is always a difficult task to try to predict the way the technology will move, but current trends seem to indicate that the technological advances that made the digital audio revolution possible will next be applied to the video side of the media. Perhaps the next edition of this book will need to be re-titled the *PC Music and Video Handbook* as integrated audio and video non-linear editors take over the market.

The Palo Alto Research Centre – which was instrumental in developing the graphical user interfaces embodied in most modern operating systems – saw the final goal of DTP development as the 'DynaBook'. This is a device about the size of a paperback book that would satisfy all the needs currently addressed by DTP packages, being able to store, process and retrieve information on demand. The musical equivalent of this would be the 'DynaStudio', a small package that could record, mix and replay music. Several systems seem to be pursuing this goal, for instance you can use the Digidesign Session-8 – coupled with a sequencer – to give you a complete music production system based on a PC and a small rack system for the interfaces and external effects units. Very soon, the musical equivalent of DTP – DTA, desk top audio – will enable anyone to produce professional music recordings from their back bedroom.

Purchase checklist

Before attempting to purchase an audio system it is important to consider how you are going to use it. You could buy a perfectly functional audio system that is totally useless for your purposes. Also check that your computer is capable of coping with the hardware and software concerned.

1 Check compatibility of your existing hardware with the software/hardware package you intend to run.

2 Consider whether your recordings requirements are better served by external hardware, i.e. a synthesiser, sound module or tape-based system may be more suitable for your purposes. For instance if you need to record in various locations a PC-based system may not be ideal.

3 If MIDI is important, check the type of interface included. Is there a Windows device driver available? SoundBlaster type cards need a special cable that connects to the joystick port; is one included/available?

4 Listen to the audio quality, is it adequate for you needs?

5 Check that your computer is compatible with your preferred system. Lap-top computers may not have an expansion slot, or may not be able to take full length cards. Note that there are currently no MCA (PS/2 micro-channel architecture) sound-cards and very few PCI devices.

6 For sampling/hard disk editing applications ensure that your computer is of sufficient power and speed to cope.

7 Check what software or tools are available for programming your own sounds and creating your own music.

8 Check the price!

7

The Windows multimedia PC

A new musical dimension

The release of the Windows 3.0 graphical user interface or GUI (goo-wee) was an example of that rare marvel, the type that causes marketing people to have hot flushes, namely a piece of software that is so good that people will buy hardware just to be able to run it. This enthusiastic response to the initial release of Windows caught almost everybody on the hop, including Microsoft, who allegedly had to redirect resources from OS/2 development to keep up with demand.

The release of Windows 3.1 in April 1992 was designed to follow up on the original success of 3.0, tidying up a number of rough edges and adding new facilities. There is no doubt that the integration of 'multimedia' facilities into the operating system was designed to promote the PC as a publishing platform, competing with such media players as Phillips's CD-I and Commodore's CDTV. In fact, superficially, the three platforms seem to have pretty similar capabilities being based on the marriage of CD and video technology, with MIDI and sound thrown in for good measure. However, the PC has an advantage in that it can be used as both a target player for multimedia publications (or 'titles') and as a production tool for creating the titles.

The audio services that are included in the operating system to support multimedia playback also provide the 'hooks' needed by any piece of music/sound software to operate on the PC. When this is combined with a mature PC music software scene and the phenomenal success of Windows 3 as a general computing operating environment, we have all the ingredients we need to produce a revolution in the use of the PC in music. This is undoubtedly why the PC is now the most popular computing platform for making music – at least if we go by the sales figures. It also explains why software companies that traditionally supported only the Mac and the Atari ST are falling over themselves to produce versions of their software that can run under Windows.

In purely practical terms, the integration of the audio services into the operating system benefits both the hardware and the software vendors. It allows the software writers to concentrate on their business, which is to produce music software, without being forced to support features (or bugs?) of the X, Y or Z MIDI interface. It helps the hardware manufacturers since they are no longer held ransom to an ageing *de facto* hardware standard. In both cases, the producers can afford to be more creative, or at least concentrate on their field of competence.

Music and sound in Windows

The basis of all the multimedia support features really boils down to 'device independence' and 'extendibility'. Device independence is actually one of the primary reasons behind any type of operating system, although you normally think of this in terms of disk drives, video display units and printers. You would be considerably put out if you had to have a particular make of printer before you could use your word processor. Why should the treatment of MIDI processors (i.e. sequencers) or sound editors be different?. Extendibility means that, as the hardware improves the operating system can easily be updated to take advantage of the new features.

In Windows 3.1, MIDI and sound are now right there in the operating system. This means that one of the biggest bugbears of writing software for the PC has now disappeared. No longer do you have to write drivers into your software to get the best out of the available PC MIDI interfaces. Why, you can even write digital sound editing software which is independent of the actual hardware and expect it to work. This is entirely due to the fact that under Windows there is a well defined and complete software interface to the various elements of the computer system that make a cheerful noise.

Windows provides both high-level and low-level access to audio services via the operating system. High-level access is designed to be used by multimedia software, and provides the ability to play MIDI sequences, sound files and even CD audio, by use of the Media Control Interface (MCI). The low-level functions give the software more precise control of the audio services and would be used by music production software. These low-level services allow you to receive and send individual MIDI messages and MIDI system exclusive data, to play and record sample data, to alter sample playback pitch and so on.

Under Windows the software can determine what sound devices are available and their individual capabilities (e.g. number of voices, sample formats supported etc.). There is also a pseudo device – called the MIDI Mapper in Windows 3.1 – that enables users to control the destination of the MIDI data streams and to re-map the program change messages to suit their particular (or even peculiar) MIDI set-up. You can even specify the drum mapping if you want.

Windows timing issues

Apart from the actual physical elements of making music with the PC, one important point that we have to consider is the temporal element, i.e. timing. If you are dealing with the performance of music then you need to have an accurate way of recording the time relationships of the various elements of the music. This accurate time-base must either be available within the computer or from outside, to allow synchronisation with external events. The operating system provides two different ways of getting timing information. You can either use the internal timer interrupt services that give you accuracy down to a millisecond (~500 ppqn at 120bpm) or use one of the device drivers to give the time in terms of SMPTE/EBU timecode, milliseconds, MIDI song position pointer or even audio samples. If you are using the latter method, the formats available and the accuracy of the timing data will depend on the capabilities of the driver, and ultimately the hardware.

Timing becomes an important issue in a multitasking software environment as there could be a number of independent and therefore asynchronous processes (i.e. applications) competing for the use of the processor. This means that a MIDI or audio application may not be 'running' the particular instant that a MIDI or audio event occurs, and thus will not be detected until that application is next scheduled. This situation is catered for by the interrupt handlers associated with the MIDI and audio device drivers. In the case of MIDI the incoming data can be time stamped when it arrives – interrupting the current application – so the error won't be apparent. On playback the situation is different; for normal MIDI playback, the application has to wait till it is scheduled before it can send a message. Thus for MIDI output under Windows, there will be an element of inaccuracy due to task swapping which will add a jitter to the timing of a MIDI sequencer. The faster the PC, the smaller these inaccuracies will be.

Windows 95

Despite the hype associated with the release of Windows 95, the differences between it and its predecessor are either superficial or buried so deep in the operating system that they are not particularly obvious. Many features in Windows 95 have been available for some time as add-ons, one of the major benefits is that Microsoft have integrated the concepts into one robust whole. If – as was rumoured – Opcode's OMS technology had been incorporated into Windows 95 initial release, the new operating system would have been a real quantum leap. As it is, musicians can take advantage of the improvements in the operating environment without changing the way they work.

One of the features of Windows 95 is the improvement of the multi-tasking of applications over its predecessor. As the new operating system is somewhat 'stricter' over how it doles out the available processing time, music applications might see an increase in the average latency on MIDI output, making playback less accurate. The early indications are that – at least for digital audio applications – performance is improved, undoubtedly due to the improved disk access methods. Any performance degradation – or enhancement – is likely to be marginal.

There is a certain amount of anecdotal evidence that the performance of certain music applications is adversely affected when run under Windows 95, but the problem can usually be traced back to the hardware (e.g. soundcard) device drivers. An inherent weakness in any system that relies on software from a number of sources is that it is only as robust as the weakest component. So look carefully at the hardware you use in your PC. Choosing a good manufacturer with local support could save you a lot of trouble with compatibility problems.

The role of the CD

Probably the biggest advance in storage technology since the first edition of this book is the widespread take-up of the CD-ROM as a form of permanent data storage. Under Windows the CD-ROM drive is a dual-purpose device that can both read CD-ROMs and play CD audio discs. Thus there are two 'musical' uses that it can be put to. The first is simply to act as a read-only data disk for loading samples or other data onto your PC's hard disk. There is a growing body of data disks that contain either MPC data files (WAV and MID files) or information specific to a particular soundcard. For example both the Gravis UltraSound and the Creative Labs AWE cards have commercial CDs available containing sound banks and optimised MIDI files designed to be played on their associated soundcards.

Another use for the attached CD player is to use it as a source of sound samples for inclusion in your music or multimedia application. As audio capabilities become more common in sequencing packages, the CD becomes an ever more convenient source of fresh audio, especially if you have limited recording facilities. The PC-based musician can take advantage of the large number of audio CDs on the market designed to be used by recording musicians, rap artists and DJs. There are two ways to get the audio off the CD onto your hard disk; recording through the soundcard's mixer, or directly reading the audio data off the disk (also called 'ripping' the audio data) The first method is just a matter of selecting the CD audio output as the recording input of the soundcard and then using any standard recording Windows application. If it is not possible to do this internally then it is a simple matter to connect the headphone output of the CD-ROM drive to the line-in on the audio card. The playback of the CD can be controlled by any standard CD audio player software.

The second method will work only on certain CD-ROM drives that implement the capability of reading raw audio from the CD. Using a piece of software like AL Digital's CD-Grab application, the audio CD can treated as a CD-ROM and the audio data can be read directly off the disk into a file on the PC's hard disk. This operation can take significantly longer than using the direct recording method and may fail if the disk is damaged in any way (or even just dirty) but the quality will be as good the original master without any of the conversion artefacts that may otherwise occur during the recording process.

One final way to use the CD in a sequencing application is to replay the audio back under the control of a music sequencer. This is possible due to the fact that the CD player operation can be controlled by software, either using low level Windows API calls (Application Programming Interface) or high level MCI (Machine Control Interface) calls. Very few Windows applications use this facility although any sequencer that allows you to embed MCI commands in the sequence can be made to control the CD. The only application that has seriously addressed this aspect of the Windows multimedia control interface is the SeqWin sequencer from Lowrie Woolf Associates, which has a definite leaning towards multimedia.

Recordable CD

Now that CD-ROM drives have come down in price to a point where almost every computer user can afford to have one, the main thrust of future development seems to be with the recordable CD (CD-R or CD-Recordable). A CD-R drive uses special blank CD-ROMs that have a gold appearance – and are thus called 'gold disks'. These disks are actually a sandwich of a gold film, an organic dye and a clear protective lacquer. The CD-R drive's laser causes the dye to change its reflective properties, giving a similar effect to the microscopic 'pits' found on a a mass produced CD (i.e. a silver disc). The upshot of this is that a gold disk can be read by a standard CD-ROM drive, making it an ideal medium for archiving (i.e. backups), distributing large amounts of data, multimedia or creating audio CDs.

Figure 7.1 The Yamaha CDE-102 CD recorder

The anatomy of an MPC soundcard

The Multimedia PC (or MPC) standard (see Appendix F) speci-fies – amongst other things – that the multimedia PC system must have a soundcard that can perform a number of audio tasks. The original MPC specification (or MPC 1) was fairly modest and reflected the cur-rent 'state of the art' games soundcards available at the time Windows 3.1 was released. The minimum requirement for the digital audio side consisted of an 8-bit digital-to-analogue converter (DAC) capable of processing waveform-audio files recorded at 22.05 and 11.025 kHz sampling rates and an 8-bit analogue-to-digital converter (ADC) capable of recording waveform-audio files at the sample rate of 11.025 kHz through an external source, such as a microphone. The internal syn-thesiser capabilities were set at a four or nine multi-voice, multitimbral capacity with two simultaneous percussive notes, which could be satis-fied by the basic AdLib (OPL 2) 'standard'.

The music side of MPC 1 was so basic that it wasn't much use for multimedia or for serious music making, but as PC audio technology developed the standard was improved to MPC 2. The digital audio side was improved to 16-bit converters with mandatory sample rates of 44.1, 22.05, and 11.025 kHz and stereo channels. The internal syn-thesiser capabilities were still pretty basic with only six simultaneous melody notes plus two simultaneous percussive notes being required, this fitting in with the SoundBlaster (or OPL 3) sound standard, again not a lot of use for music making. Neither MPC 1 or 2 make the inclu-sion of a MIDI port mandatory but the next revision (MPC 3) looks set to make this a requirement.

The MPC standard is currently in the throes of being improved again to upgrade the digital audio performance and include a wavetable capability on the internal synthesis. The minimum internal synthesiser capabilities are still very modest with the multi-voice, multi-timbral capacity of six simultaneous melody voices plus two simultane-ous percussive voices being still very low especially when you consider the 24-voice requirement of General MIDI and Roland's GS standard.

It makes you wonder whether the MPC committee really under-stand the music side of the specification since two percussive voices are not even enough for the most basic of drum kits (bass drum/snare drum/hi-hat). While most MPC 3 soundcards will have much higher polyphony – in line with the GM requirement – it is important to check the specification of any card that you plan to purchase, since it may satisfy the MPC 3 standard but be virtually useless for serious MIDI sequencing. Another item lacking from the MPC 3 specification is a requirement to record and play back digital audio simultaneously, which is a necessity if you want to use the card in a hard disk recording system

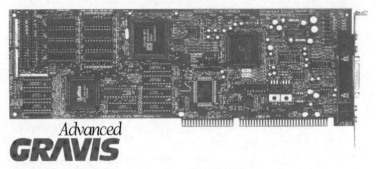

Figure 7.2(a) The Gravis UltraSound MAX MPC Soundcard

Figure 7.2(b) MPC audio cards like the Turtle Beach Tahiti turn your PC into a digital recording studio

MPC sound capabilities

There are any number of soundcards available for the IBM PC (or ISA) family of personal computers that conform to the MPC (i.e. Multimedia PC) audio standard. However there is a lot of confusion about what the miscellaneous capabilities mean. So here's a concise definition of what the various bits do, and what software you can use to get a sound out of your PC.

Hardware	Software	Production tips
OPL3 (FM) based synthesiser [aka. SB Pro]	MIDI sequencer	There's not a lot you can do with this except make semi-musical noises. Ideal if you want your music to sound like it has been created on a Stylophone
ROM based wavetable synthesiser	MIDI sequencer	Useful for producing orchestrations or demos using 'standard' instruments.
RAM based wavetable synthesiser	MIDI sequencer, sample editor	This type of card can be used for creating personalised sounds to give your music a unique flavour. You can also sample short segments of music and use the sequencer to loop the sample to give a 'break beat'.
8-bit digital audio replay	MOD file editor and player	A MOD file uses short samples to produce the sound, transposing them on-the-fly to give the tune. Some of these are very impressive but the editing interface for creating these is usually pretty primitive.
16-bit digital audio replay	Direct to disk recording (D2D)	Use your hard disk as a sound storage medium, effectively turning your PC into a tape recorder. The number of tracks will depend on the power of your PC/soundcard combination (some cards have independent processing power) and the software you use unless you use specialist HD recording hardware like the Session-8 or Soundscape SSDHR-1. With a Pentium you could expect to get up to 8 tracks. To record multiple tracks successfully, your soundcard needs to be able to record and play back simultaneously, or some software allows you to use two soundcards.

| External MIDI | MIDI sequencer, synthesiser. 'voice' editors, sample editors | This allows you to use your PC to control a MIDI studio and act as a central control centre and network hub. As well as making music you can use the system to design synthesiser and sampler sounds, downloading the sounds to the external modules via MIDI or SCSI. |
| Dedicated hard disk recorder | Proprietary software supplied with hardware | Use your PC as a high spec. digital multitrack recorder. The use of additional hardware gets around any PC data throughput limitations. The facilities offered are limited only by the hardware chosen – and your budget. These systems invariably require that you buy dedicated disk storage for your audio data. |

Setting up your MPC sound system

The core of the Windows 3.1x MIDI control section is the MIDI Mapper. This facility determines the default behaviour of MIDI when accessed by a Windows application. Most MIDI sequencers either don't use the MIDI Mapper or simply provide it as an option, but multimedia software almost always uses it to control the MIDI device connected to the PC. Also any software that uses the Media Control Interface (i.e. MCI) will also use the MIDI Mapper to define how the MIDI data is going to be interpreted. The MIDI Mapper – which is accessed using the icon in the Control Panel – is actually quite a powerful tool for letting you play General MIDI song files using a combination of older or otherwise non-GM MIDI synthesisers. The MIDI Mapper has three sections:

1 Set-ups for matching the instruments to the MIDI channels
2 Patch maps for matching your non-GM patch set to MPC
3 Key maps mainly for matching drum sounds to GM, but also useful for shifting instruments up or down an octave for non-standard (usually Yamaha) note mappings

To alter any of these settings you need to activate the MIDI Mapper control icon from the Windows Control Panel. Before you can consider creating a new patch map for your synthesiser(s) you need to use the Setups 'page' to match MIDI channels to your external modules. Two things to remember here are that the lower numbered MIDI channels are always used first (so you want to have the best sounds here) and that the GM drums sounds appear on MIDI channel 10. So, for instance, if you have a home keyboard with drum sounds played on MIDI channel 16 you will need to set the destination for channel 10 of

Figure 7.3 Select the MIDI mapper from the Windows control panel

the MIDI file to channel 16 on your sound module (i.e. 'Dest Chan' = 16 for 'Src Chan' 10). You then need to set up a patch map to convert the General MIDI sound programs to match your MIDI set-up. This is mainly done using the 'patch maps' and possibly the 'key maps' sections of the MIDI Mapper.

You will need the following:

- a list of the GM patch set with the program numbers
- a list of the patches/program numbers for your external MIDI gear
- a list of the MIDI channels that your synthesiser can receive on (often described as the multitimbrality)

you may also need:

- a list of the GM drum mapping
- a list of the drum mapping for your MIDI synthesiser

Steps:

1 Draw up a chart that relates the sound in your synthesiser module to the equivalent GM sound. e.g.

MPC/GM patch	Your synthesiser module
1 Acoustic piano	23 Piano 1
2 Bright piano	23 Piano 1
3 Electric grand	24 Fender Rhodes
etc...	

Note:

The numbers relate to the 'program' numbers. You may find that in your instrument/module documents they start from '0' instead of '1'. If so just click on the "1-based patches" button in the patch map window to make them start at 0 (zero). (You may have to use your imagination to match up the sounds and/or repeat sounds if there isn't a direct match.)

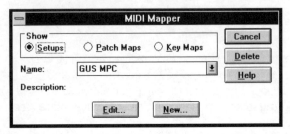

Figure 7.4 Click on 'New' to create a custom Windows MIDI configuration

2 Use the patch maps section of the MIDI Mapper to create a new map that will select an appropriate sound on your synthesiser when Windows sends out a GM patch number.

Src Patch	Src Patch Name	Dest Patch	Volume %	Key Map Name
0	Acoustic Grand Piano	0	100	[None]
1	Bright Acoustic Piano	1	100	+1 octave
2	Electric Grand Piano	3	100	[None]
3	Honky-tonk Piano	7	100	MT32
4	Rhodes Piano	5	100	21
5	Chorused Piano	6	100	+2 octaves
6	Harpsichord	17	100	MT32
7	Clavinet	21	100	small_drumkit
8	Celesta	22	100	[None]
9	Glockenspiel	101	100	[None]
10	Music Box	101	100	[None]
11	Vibraphone	98	100	[None]
12	Marimba	104	100	[None]
13	Xylophone	103	100	[None]
14	Tubular Bells	102	100	[None]
15	Dulcimer	105	100	[None]

MIDI Patch Map: 'MT32' — 1 based patches — 256k_drums

Figure 7.5 Use the patch map screen to associate the Windows program numbers with those on your MIDI module

3 Use the setups section of the MIDI Mapper to associate the new patch map with MIDI channels that your synthesiser can receive on. You need to select a port for each of the 16 MIDI channels. If your external sound module can handle more than one channel at a time – i.e. is multitimbral – it will appear more than once on the list. Remember that the lower channels are used the most so connect these to your best MIDI sound modules.

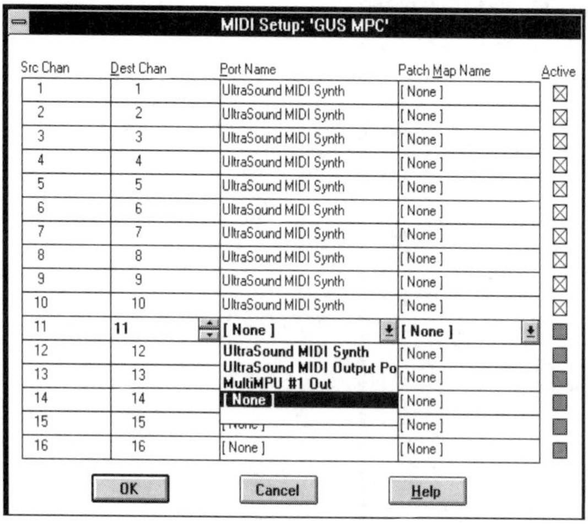
MIDI Setup: 'GUS MPC'

Src Chan	Dest Chan	Port Name	Patch Map Name	Active
1	1	UltraSound MIDI Synth	[None]	☒
2	2	UltraSound MIDI Synth	[None]	☒
3	3	UltraSound MIDI Synth	[None]	☒
4	4	UltraSound MIDI Synth	[None]	☒
5	5	UltraSound MIDI Synth	[None]	☒
6	6	UltraSound MIDI Synth	[None]	☒
7	7	UltraSound MIDI Synth	[None]	☒
8	8	UltraSound MIDI Synth	[None]	☒
9	9	UltraSound MIDI Synth	[None]	☒
10	10	UltraSound MIDI Synth	[None]	☒
11	11	[None]	[None]	
12	12	UltraSound MIDI Synth	[None]	
13	13	UltraSound MIDI Output Po	[None]	
14	14	MultiMPU #1 Out	[None]	
15	15	[None]	[None]	
16	16	[None]	[None]	

OK Cancel Help

Figure 7.6 Now use the setup dialogue to associate your sound module with a particular MIDI channel

If your synth's percussion/drum kit section doesn't use the Roland or GM drum mapping, you will need to work out how its drum note numbers are related to the GM sounds. Middle C (C3) is note number 60 (or 3C hex), so you can count down (or up) by 'walking' chromatically across the keys until you hit the sound you want. More steps:

4 Draw up a chart that relates the drum sounds on your synthesiser module to the equivalent GM sound. e.g.

MPC/GM drum sound		Your synthesiser module	
36	bass drum	23	kick drum 1
37	side stick	44	rim shot [1]
38	acoustic snare	25	snare
	etc		

Again you may have to use your imagination to match up the sound and/or repeat sounds if there isn't a match for the GM drum sounds.

5 Use the key maps section of the MIDI Mapper to create a new map that will select the right drum sound on your synthesiser when Windows sends out a GM drum note number.

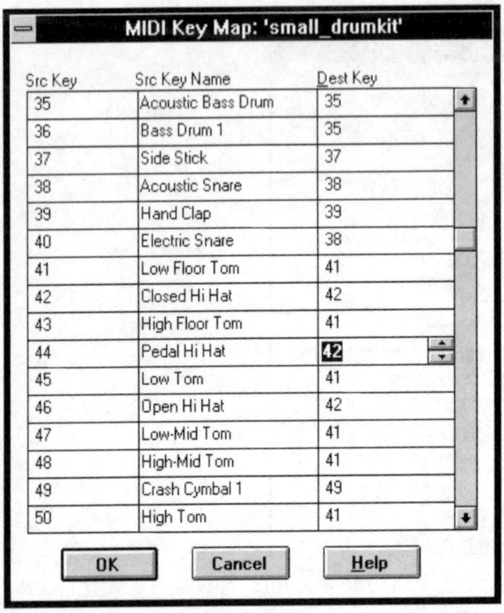

Src Key	Src Key Name	Dest Key	
35	Acoustic Bass Drum	35	↑
36	Bass Drum 1	35	
37	Side Stick	37	
38	Acoustic Snare	38	
39	Hand Clap	39	
40	Electric Snare	38	
41	Low Floor Tom	41	
42	Closed Hi Hat	42	
43	High Floor Tom	41	
44	Pedal Hi Hat	42	
45	Low Tom	41	
46	Open Hi Hat	42	
47	Low-Mid Tom	41	
48	High-Mid Tom	41	
49	Crash Cymbal 1	49	
50	High Tom	41	↓

MIDI Key Map: 'small_drumkit'

OK   Cancel   Help

Figure 7.7 You may also need to re-map your drum sounds to match the MPC/GM standard

6 Assign the new key map to the first row (i.e. patch) in a new patch maps page created for the drum/percussion channel and associate this to MIDI channel 10 in the setups page of the MIDI Mapper. Don't forget to set the destination channel to the MIDI channel(s) that your synthesiser's percussion section uses (usually 10 or 16).

You can create different drum maps by creating new Key Maps and then associating them with different rows in the Patch Maps page that you've created for your drum channel. If you are creating your own MIDI sequences you can then select between the different drum maps by selecting the appropriate program on the percussion channel. Unfortunately you can't copy the contents of one mapping to a new one so you will need to start from scratch each time you want to add a new instrument, but you shouldn't have to do it too often.

Windows 95

Under Windows 95 the MIDI functions have been simplified somewhat in that there is no 'built-in' facility to edit the patch maps and drum maps. This simplification is no doubt due to the greater prevalence of GM compatible soundcards and external MIDI modules than when Windows 3.1 was first introduced. It is far less likely that a PC user will want to cobble together such a system from individual components. The default MIDI set-up is controlled from the MIDI sheet of the multimedia properties dialogue, which is accessed from the Windows 95 Control Panel. There are two basic modes; either you can direct the MIDI to a single instrument – say a soundcard or a sound module attached to a MIDI port – or you can use the Custom configuration to direct each MIDI channel to (potentially) a different sound module or just switch it off.

Unlike the MIDI Mapper in Windows 3 there is no direct way of editing the mapping of the MPC General MIDI sound set so that it will select different sounds on the external sound module. However you can

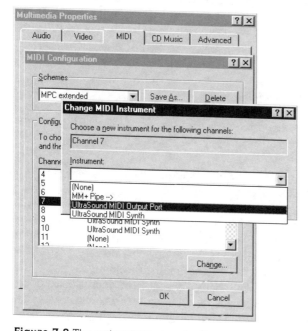

Figure 7.8 The custom setup screen allows you to associate a module with a particular MIDI channel

do the same thing by creating an IDF (instrument definition file) and then associating it to a MIDI port using the 'advanced' sheet of the multimedia properties dialogue. Microsoft intended that these files should be supplied by the manufacturer of the sound module (or MIDI keyboard). So that you can customise these mappings or create new ones for MIDI instruments that are no longer supported, Microsoft have also made an editor available (called IDFEDIT) which allows you to create your own instrument definitions.

As a single IDF file can contain descriptions for more than one instrument, you can actually use this mechanism to 'customise' your PC's MIDI set-up. So you could create one file that describes all your instruments; for example, a wavetable synthesiser with several memory configurations, an external MIDI keyboard with built-in sound etc. One interesting application would be to use the IDF mechanism to allow two PC based musicians to make their MIDI set-ups compatible – say for collaborating on a song. The IDFEDIT application should be available from most music or Windows based bulletin boards (e.g. the Windows 95 forum on Compuserve) or you could try your local Microsoft support organisation.

To customise an IDF you can either start with a new file, or modify an existing file, if you are just 'tweaking' your current set-up. Like the Windows 3.1 process described above you will need to define the program mapping first.

You will need the following:

- a list of the GM patch set with the program numbers
- a list of the patches/program numbers for your external MIDI gear
- a list of the MIDI channels that your synthesiser can receive on (often described as the multitimbrality)

To edit an instrument double click on it (or select it and click on the 'properties' button). After checking that the 'ID' and 'Info' sheets are accurate, select the 'patch map' sheet by clicking on its tab. Now select each row in turn and edit the 'map to' column to match the patch mapping for your MIDI module/keyboard (cf. your module documentation). This is quite a tedious task, but at least you only have to do it once, since you can copy the configuration between different maps using the copy/paste functions – accessible by clicking on the selected instruments using the right-hand mouse button. To re-map the pitches you use the key map rather than the patch map. For instance, if you want your sounds to play back an octave higher than the default values then you need to add 12 to each of the current values in the 'map to' column. Incidentally, in both of these maps, any values that remain unchanged from the MPC GM standard are marked with an asterisk.

Figure 7.9(a) The IDF editor allows you to create your own custom patch maps

If you need to set-up a drum module, then first use the 'channels' sheet to select which MIDI channel the module receives percussion on and then use the 'percussion map' sheet to map each individual drum to its GM equivalent. Any channels that are not used should be muted. You will need:

- a list of the GM drum mapping (i.e. drum type vs. MIDI note value)
- a list of the drum mapping for your MIDI synthesiser

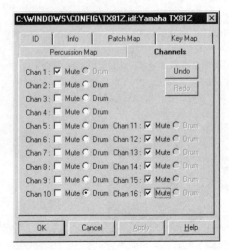

Figure 7.9(b) Use the channels sheet to define the tone generator's MIDI configuration

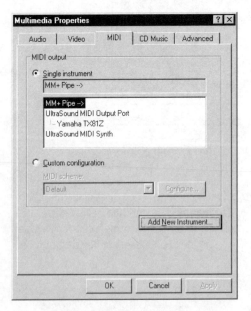

Figure 7.9(c) Associate an instrument to a port using the MIDI section of the multimedia properties dialogue

You can create a 'template' IDF file for each instrument in your MIDI set-up and then use the copy/paste mechanism to create IDF files with multiple instruments. Simply start up a new IDF editor page for each of the templates and then 'copy' each instrument into your working IDF file.

When you've completed the edit, you need to utilise the 'add new instrument' button before you can use it. Use the 'remove' button on the 'properties' sheet of the multimedia properties dialogue (accessed via the 'advanced' sheet) to remove an instrument (i.e. IDF) from a particular port. To use the instrument select it on the 'MIDI' sheet, either by selecting it from the 'single instrument' list or as part of a 'custom' set-up (Figure 7.9(c)).

The audio side has been improved considerably with both the ability to handle a wide range of different WAV file formats and has the ability to convert between source and playback formats 'on the fly'. Using the Audio sheet on the Multimedia Properties dialogue, you can

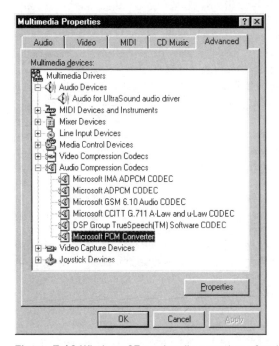

Figure 7.10 Windows 95 can handle a number of audio compression formats

define the playback resolution that Windows uses when recording sounds – say when making voice annotations – so that you can optimise performance and disk space used. The support of system sounds – i.e. noises the computer makes when something happens in Windows – is much improved but doesn't really make much difference to the musical user of the PC.

Sound production for multimedia

A more reliable music format for multimedia applications is the digital audio sound file. The main advantage of this over MIDI is that the sound the user hears doesn't rely on the quality or capability of the synthesiser on the MPC soundcard. While soundcards do have different digital audio capabilities the variation won't be as extreme as the difference between, say, an OPL3 synthesiser found on a basic MPC 1 soundcard and an advanced wavetable synthesiser on, for instance, a Creative Labs AWE-32. The quality may not be as good as a good MIDI-based card, but at least it will sound better than the buzzes and beeps that characterise a basic FM card. This doesn't mean that you must discard your high quality MIDI synthesiser when developing sound for multimedia applications, it just means that you have to record the results as a WAV file rather than use the MIDI data file directly.

There are two issues that must be addressed when using digital audio files in a multimedia environment. The first is that digital audio data takes up a lot more disk space than the equivalent MIDI file. A modestly specified sound file (22kHz, 8-bit stereo) will be over 100 times the size of the equivalent MIDI file. The other issue is that older MPC 1 based PCs may not be able to play files that have a resolution higher than 8 bits, or a sample rate greater than 22 kHz. These factors mean that commercial Windows multimedia applications tend to stick to fairly conservative quality standards to be compatible with the greatest number of target systems. There are also compressed audio formats – such as ADPCM – that are enhancements to the original Windows audio specification and can give significant space savings, but suffer from the same problem as high quality sound files – older systems may not be able to play the sounds.

Since most hard disk recording systems work at CD quality – 16 bit samples at 44.1 kHz sample rate, the audio will need to be converted to a more compact data format before it can be delivered as part of your final multimedia project. Most MPC based systems will have the option of saving the audio either at a lower resolution or in a different format. If not, then there are a large number of conversion utilities available – either commercially or as shareware – that allow you to process the audio file. One good example of this kind of program is ReSample from Audio Morphology which supports a wide range of audio formats – including some for samplers – and can process a batch of files.

There are a few simple points that you need to consider when producing these lower resolution audio files for use in the Windows or multimedia environment. The first is that you should make good use of the dynamic range of the sample format you have chosen (i.e. don't record the sound at too low a level), as the perceived noise of a sample is a constant value and dependent on the number bits in the sample format. So for an eight-bit sample the maximum number of discrete levels that can be used to describe the waveform is 256, giving a quantisation error of half the step size (i.e. one 512th). These quantisation errors are perceived as 'noise' while the sound is playing and – since it is a constant value – will appear to be larger if the sound is at a lower

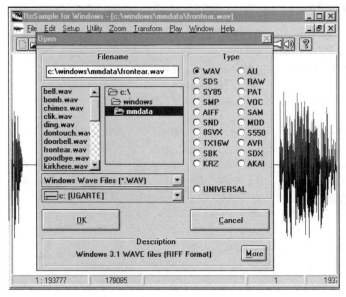

Figure 7.11 Sample files can be easily converted to more suitable formats using one of the many Windows audio conversion utilities

overall level. Another technique to minimise the effect of this quantisation noise is to add a low level noise signal to the final mix to 'swamp' the quantisation noise – so it is no longer signal dependent but constant. This may seem like a strange thing to do, but the human ear (or brain) tends to screen out constant level signals so the noise is actually less obvious than the lower level, but varying quantisation noise signal.

Another point to consider is that the frequency response – or rather the highest frequency that can be reproduced – is reduced when the sample rate is reduced. The highest frequency that can be recorded is half the sample rate, so a CD can theoretically reproduce frequencies up to 22.05 kHz, while at a sample rate of 11.025 kHz the highest frequency is reduced to just over 5.5 kHz. While the recording or conversion process will discard the frequencies above this cut-off point (known as the Nyquist point), the authors' experience has shown that some unpleasant side effects can occur. The most obvious is with female speech where the 'ss' sound becomes a 'sh' – so for instance the word "missile" becomes "mishile" and so on. This unwanted effect can be avoided by band-limiting the signal's frequency response before the conversion is performed, usually by using the digital equalisation built into most decent sample or non-linear editing software.

MPC MIDI files

Sometimes you may have no choice but to use MIDI – possibly due to storage constraints. There are some techniques that you can use to help you get the best possible results from a wide range of soundcard capabilities.

The committee that developed the MPC standard for Windows realised that there was a wide variation in the quality of soundcards installed in PCs and so they designed this fact into the Windows MIDI specification. As MIDI can control up to 16 instruments, they designated the top four as a basic sound set (MIDI channels 13 to 16) and the lower ten (i.e. MIDI channels 1-10) as the extended set; channels 11 and 12 are not used in this scheme. The 'basic' set-up is modelled on the AdLib/SoundBlaster FM soundcard while the 'extended' set is loosely based on the Roland LA-PC synthesiser card.

This might all sound pretty complicated, but the idea behind it is that you can store two arrangements of the same composition into one MIDI file. You can then select between the two arrangements by muting the appropriate tracks using the Windows MIDI Mapper. Most soundcards will come with a number of pre-programmed MIDI Mapper configurations that are optimised for either the basic or extended sound sets. So you can author a MIDI file in such a way that it will play properly on either type of card; the file may not sound particularly pleasing using the basic set-up, but at least it won't sound ridiculous.

MIDI channel	Description	Polyphony
1 – 9	extended melodic tracks	16 notes
10	extended percussion track	16 notes
11 and 12	[not used]	
13 – 15	base-level melodic tracks	six notes
16	base-level percussion track	three notes

As you can see from the table, in the extended set channel 10 is the drum channel – which is the same as General MIDI (i.e. GM and GS) – and channel 16 is used in the basic set. So if you play a Windows MIDI file on a GM sound module or soundcard it will usually sound pretty awful since the basic drum track will be playing on a pitched instrument.

On the other hand if you play a General MIDI file using the Windows media player, you will either get missing tracks or complete garbage depending on whether the PC has an extended or basic sound set.

To take account of this non-standard (in MIDI terms) file format, the MCI sequencer – which is the MIDI player 'engine' – checks to see if the MIDI files are marked with a 'signature' that indicates that the files have been created for use with Windows. The first time you try to play a non-Windows file using the media player a warning dialogue box will pop-up to tell you that the file may not sound as intended by the composer. This message can be permanently disabled by clicking on the 'Don't display this warning in future' check box.

As the MCI sequencer is used by most multimedia player software, you need to be aware that this message will probably occur when the first MIDI file is played. From experience we've found that this kind of warning message will cause angst in all but the most hardened Windows user. The easiest way to avoid this is to create MIDI files that adhere to the standard, both by using the track structure defined above and by marking the file as Windows compatible. This won't ensure that your MIDI files will work in every situation, as soundcards are notorious for screwing around with the MIDI Mapper, but at least you'll have best possible chance of getting it right.

This is not really the place to give details on how to create a MIDI file but there are a few points to watch out for. The easiest way to create or modify a MIDI score for Windows is to sort out the extended arrangement first (i.e. channels 1 to 10) and then remove material to make it work with the basic set-up. The main thing you need to watch is that you don't run out of notes as the polyphony on both types of set-up is limited. Polyphony refers to the maximum number of notes that the soundcard can play at any one time.

So for instance, with the basic synthesiser you can have a maximum of only six melodic notes and three drum sounds playing simultaneously, compared to the 16 available with the extended specification. Once the file sounds all right, mark it as a Windows MIDI file.

Microsoft provide a utility called MARKMIDI.EXE as part of the Windows SDK, and it can also be found as part of various language products such as Visual C++. It is a DOS program that marks a MIDI file with a Microsoft meta-event to indicate that the file is compatible with the Microsoft MIDI authoring guidelines. The invocation syntax is:

MARKMIDI source destination

where   source   specifies the MIDI file to be marked
        destination   specifies the filename for the marked file

According to the Microsoft Product support line this file is redistributable so may be available on on-line services such as CIX or Compuserve. Another way of producing marked MIDI files is to use the Windows version of the Cakewalk Professional sequencer which provides the marking function as an option when you save your sequence as a MIDI file.

The moving image

As the power of the PC increases, more and more people are looking to it to start manipulating video images. There are a number of different ways you can use the PC in the video domain, for instance you can use the PC to control external devices such as VTR machines, effectively replacing the traditional edit controller. At the other end of the spectrum, you can use the PC to perform the actual editing, by digitising the images onto your hard disk and then using non-linear editor software like Adobe Premier.

How the PC is used for video rather depends on what the end product is going to be. For instance the latter of the above options is ideal for producing digital video for inclusion in multimedia presentations etc., but you can't get the quality required for broadcast (or even low band) applications. So if your video is going to end up on someone's TV, then you have to stick to traditional methods, however if your images are going to end on a computer screen somewhere then it is definitely worth looking at a digital editing system.

The 'native' video format Windows is the AVI standard which stands for Audio and Video Interleaved. As the name implies, the video frames and sound track audio are interleaved, making the synchronisation of sound to image implicit. The standard supports various video compression algorithms, dependent on the Windows drivers installed, giving the possibility of hardware support for particular application. Another popular format is based on the MPEG 1 and 2 video standards which give superior compression ratios at the expense of not being able to edit the finished video.

The first thing you need to do is to get the video onto your hard disk. To do this you need to have a video capture card – for instance the RT300 VideoBlaster from Creative Labs. Since the PC is not really up to replaying digital video at high resolutions or frame rate, compression techniques are used to reduce the load on the PC's processor. The better cards will incorporate hardware video compression technology to both give the highest possible quality at capture, and reduce the amount of hard disk space taken up by the digitised video.

Ideally the capture card should digitise the moving video images, compress them in 'real-time' and then save the video – as an AVI file – onto your hard disk as a single process. For instance the RT300 card uses a hardware implementation of the Indeo compression system – based around an Intel i750 processor – which gives a compression

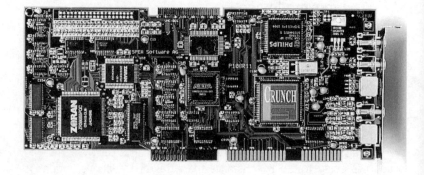

Figure 7.12(a) You need to install a dedicated video capture card like
this SPEA Crunchit card to get the best results.

ratio of 6:1 and can handle frame sizes up to 320x240 and frame
rates up to 30 fps (frames per second)

The capture card should come with Video for Windows drivers
that should let you use the card with any compatible capture software.
Capture cards quite often come with bundled software that will allow
you to both capture and edit the video data. It should allow you to
choose the frame size, frame rate and compression ratio as well as
choose between a number of capture methods, including normal video,
single frame, step and timed capture.

Advanced features are the ability to remotely control a VCR
attached to your PC if you have an appropriate MCI device controller
installed. You should also be able to capture the audio sound track
along with the video either using a soundcard in your PC or using an
audio input on the capture card.

Video editing

A good example of a video editing package is Adobe Premiere,
which consists of a capture program (AdobeCap) and a video editing
application (Premiere). Using the Adobe software you have a wide
range of options for manipulating video on your PC. Using Premier provides a simple way to splice together your captured video clips along
with bit map graphic files and even Autodesk animation files, so you
can get a pretty decent looking video – albeit within the limitations of
video for Windows. The software can cut and fade between the

various formats with 35 different types of transition between adjacent video clips being available. Premier is capable of some quite advanced editing techniques such as superimposing images and special graphic effects. There are also three audio tracks so that you 'dub' sound to the edited video, with graphically controllable fades and cropping tools.

Premier can save the edited video in AVI or Apple Quicktime movie formats, Photoshop 'filmstrip' format or – if you have a suitable hardware and a powerful PC – print to a video tape machine. The way that this is achieved is to use either a video card that has a direct video output, or a converter that can take the output of your the PC's video card and turn it into a composite or RGB video signal. One point you

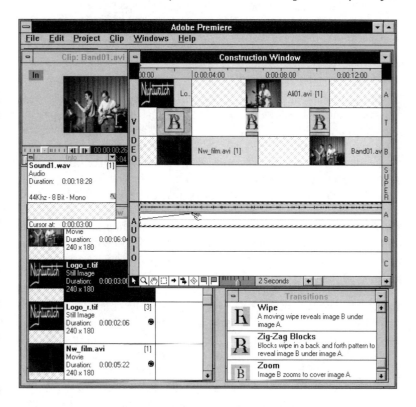

Figure 7.12(b) A nonlinear video editor like Adobe Premier gives a convenient method of integrating sound and video images

need to be aware of is that American and European video standards are different and incompatible so be sure that the product you get is suitable for your local video standard.

Programming

The Windows multimedia functions are accessible to any programmer as part of the general Windows API, which should be supplied as part of any Windows development platform. The system calls are documented in the Microsoft Windows Multimedia Programmer's Reference with examples of their use in the Microsoft Windows Multimedia Programmer's Workbook. A third book in the series the Microsoft Windows Multimedia Authoring and Tools Guide looks at the high level authoring tools and the processes involved in integrating images, sound and text data in a multimedia application (see Appendix D for details).

Authoring – putting it together

As multimedia involves taking elements from a lot of different types of media – i.e. sound, video, animation etc. – and integrating them into an application. This has given rise to a new kind of developer – the multimedia producer. The role of the multimedia producer is akin to an editor or systems integrator, taking the material from the various media producers and forging it into an integrated multimedia publication. The tools available for achieving this task are usually known as multimedia authoring tools and can vary tremendously in price and capability from simple 'point and click' applications to systems that look very much like object oriented programming environments.

The programming techniques referred to in the previous section are just as applicable to multimedia development as they are to music applications and will give greater control over how the system performs. However, authoring systems tend to be aimed more at the less technically oriented creative person and often provide a quick way of creating quite sophisticated multimedia applications. To musicians, multimedia provides an opportunity to place their music into a wider context by associating images and text with the music, facilities formerly available only to those who could afford to make a music video.

When recordable CDs come down in price enough to be considered a consumer product, then every musician will have the capability to 'publish' their own music without recourse to the music business.

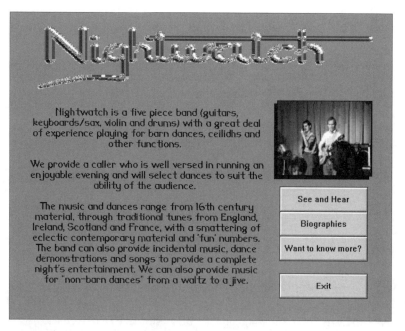

Figure 7.13 Multimedia can help the musician or the music

How this music will be distributed is a matter that only the future can reveal, however it does look like the Internet may play a big role in this quiet revolution.

Bits and PCs

The IBM PC has come a long way since it was introduced in 1981, with new variants becoming available as advances in technology make performance improvements possible. The original PC was based on the Intel 8088 microprocessor and had 64 kilobytes of RAM (expandable to 640K) and a single 5.25 inch floppy disk drive. This was followed at the beginning of 1983 with the PC/XT which had a 10 megabyte hard disk and later in the same year by the ill fated PCjr. By the end of 1984 the 80286 based PC/AT with 256 kilobytes of RAM and IBM's new high density floppy disks was available and, with its 16-bit expansion bus, gave a quantum leap in the processing power available to the personal computer user. Since then 386, 486 and Pentium based PCs with ever increasing clock speeds have become available.

PC/AT – 80286

The Intel 80286 processor was considered by many pundits as a 'stop gap' processor and has been entirely superseded by 80386, 80486 and Pentium processors for use in PC/ATs – which are commonly referred to as ISA PCs. The 80286 is essentially a faster 8086 with some added facilities for multi-tasking – unfortunately, due to a fairly fundamental flaw in the design, it was never able to reach its full potential. The shortcomings of the 286 were overcome by the introduction of the 16 bit version of the 80386 – the SX variant. The 286-based AT is inherently more powerful than the original PC, and as such, was more suitable for computer intensive tasks such as producing the high quality video graphics required for scoring applications.

You may come across these machines second hand and you could find them useful for a DOS MIDI based system or for remote control of lighting systems and such like, but they don't have the power or the graphics capabilities required by most current Windows applications. You might also find a 286-based PC/AT useful as a door stop!

PC/AT – 80386, 80486 and the Pentium

The PCs that use the Intel 80386 and later processors use the same basic architecture as the AT style PC except that they use a 32 bit processor. This extra power makes these computers eminently suitable for multi-tasking applications, especially as they do not have the problems associated with the 286 processor. For a single user system, the extra power gives faster response for advanced graphic applications such as computer aided design. This extra power is required if you want to run Windows as your operating environment, or under DOS if you have a very processor intensive application such as required by packages like CSOUND (which uses digital algorithms to generate complicated electronic instrument sounds). The 386 has virtually gone the way of the humble PC and 286 based PC/AT computers.

The meaning of the SX designation on Intel processors varies and depends on whether it is a 386 or a 486. On a 386-based machine the SX means that the external data buses are only 16 bits wide, rather than the 32 bits of the full 80386. This gives a performance penalty for any 32 bit operations since two memory accesses are required to read a single 32 bit value. On the 486, the SX designation indicates that there is no numeric co-processor built on the CPU chip, which means that there is a performance penalty when any floating point calculations are performed. MIDI applications will see little or no performance penalty due to running on an SX based PC, but digital audio applications may be affected.

Another variation on the 486 theme is the double clocked (DX2) and triple clocked (DX4) processors. These chips double (or triple) the external clock speed to improve performance, thus both DX2/66 and DX4/100 PCs use a processor clock of 33 MHz which is then multiplied on the CPU to give a higher internal clock rate. However, whenever the CPU needs to read or write data to the RAM, hard disk or an external device it must 'slow down' to the external clock rate – i.e. 33 MHz. This means that you can get substantial speed increases for repetitive calculations – such as for large spreadsheets or video applications – but not for calculations or operations that access external memory a lot.

On the buses

The single feature that has ensured the longevity of the original PC was its expansion bus. This ability to add adapter cards to the system has meant that the PC can be used for a large number of different (and disparate) applications. The original bus specification was for an eight bit data bus which was clocked at the PC's clock speed – i.e. 4.7 MHz. When the AT was introduced this bus was expanded to a 16 bit bus in a way that was still compatible with the original eight bit bus, so that all the existing cards could still be used in the new computer. This AT bus has become known as the ISA bus (Industry Standard Architecture) and is still the most commonly available bus standard on the PC. The price of backward compatibility was that the new bus was still clocked at 4.7 MHz as that was the original standard for the eight bit expansion cards. Today, most PCs can be set to increase this speed (by altering the settings used by the ROM BIOS – stored in the CMOS memory) but there is no guarantee that an ISA expansion card will operate at the higher speed, though most modern cards will.

This – now venerable – data bus is a major 'bottleneck' for any application that requires large amounts of data to be read into (and/or out of) the PC. Consider an MPC-based digital audio application, the sound data must be read off the hard disk, processed by the CPU and then sent out to the soundcard. The data is transferred across the bus twice. At the same time the soundcard may be recording audio – which also has to cross the bus twice – as well as displaying high-resolution graphics on the computer's screen. There are other data flows across the bus at the same time; mouse movements, printer output, data communications and network activity are all funnelled through this relatively slow channel, causing a kind of computing log jam.

There are two solutions to the problem currently competing for market acceptance. The VESA (or VL) bus is another extension to the AT/ISA bus that takes it up to 32 bits. Like the 16 bit enhancement to the original PC bus it adds another connector in-line with the existing 16 bit (and 8 bit) standard. While VESA cards can be very fast, they can suffer from mechanical production tolerance problems that make expansion cards difficult to insert and unreliable in operation. The main competitor is the PCI (Peripheral Chip Interconnect) bus which uses a new 32 bit connector and includes auto-configuration facilities (plug and play) into its basic design. It also has the advantage – at least for the card manufacturer – that it is a multi-platform standard.

The significance of RAM

RAM or random access memory is very important to the operation of a PC. The amount of RAM installed in a PC will determine the complexity of the applications you can run and – under Windows – how fast the machine runs. The minimum amount of memory required to run any flavour of Windows is 4 megabytes and increasing this to 8 or even 16 megabytes can put skates on your PC's performance.

Until recently, RAM came on 30 pin SIMMs (single in-line memory modules), but the growing acceptance of 32 bit operating systems like Windows NT means that these are being superseded by 72 pin SIMMs which give higher capacity and performance than their predecessors. All RAM has a rated access speed defined in nanoseconds (ns), which for most current PC's needs to be at least 70ns. SIMMs are usually fitted directly to the PC motherboard and are quite easily installed by the user, check the PC's documentation for more details.

The only other confusing point about RAM is the parity bit. When IBM first developed the PC they designed it to use nine bit RAM chips rather than the eight bit memory commonly used in most other personal computers. The extra bit is a parity or check bit that the ROM BIOS software can use to verify whether the RAM is functioning properly when it performs its power on start tests and during normal operation. The IBM designers felt that it was very important to detect errors that might be caused by a failure in the memory and not allow the corrupted data to propagate further in the system. This means that detection of a parity error causes the PC to stop dead in its tracks, which is rather extreme, but justifiable considering the circumstances. This means that you need to ask for nine bit memory when upgrading your RAM. There are eight bit SIMMs available that 'fool' the PC into thinking that a parity bit is present, but using these will remove the parity 'safety net'. Some PC motherboards can also take 8 or 9 bit SIMMs. Check your documentation before buying more RAM.

The PowerPC 'alternative'

Over the years there has been a lot of speculation about the future of personal computing and how long the Intel x86 family of processors can last before they run out of steam. In 1991 IBM, Apple and

Motorola got together to create a new personal computing standard based on a new chip made by Motorola but using RISC (reduced instruction set computer) technology developed by IBM. Back then, it looked very hopeful, with three industry giants pooling resources to produce something that wouldn't suffer from the problems inherent in the design of the PC. A *Byte* magazine editorial at the time hailed the venture as 'a move toward common systems that can ease the pangs of incompatibility'.

The new platform would be expandable like the original PC, but use the PCI bus, which would solve the throughput and installation problems in one fell swoop. Compatibility with existing programs – both PC and Apple Macintosh – would be maintained by having software emulators for both these software environments. The idea was that the new PowerPC would be so much faster that the overhead of using an extra layer of software would be cancelled out, giving comparable performance to the original platforms. This would mean that new and existing products could be converted to 'native' PowerPC code to take advantage of the new, faster hardware but most older software could still be run if the need arose.

A few years down the road things don't look particularly promising. As Jack Schofield (*Computer Guardian*) has pointed out, the IBM PowerPC and the Apple PowerMac are wholly incompatible from both a hardware and a software point of view. They may use the same processor chip but apart from that they might as well be entirely different computers. IBM has now announced that it will be working with Apple to produce a Common Hardware Reference Platform (or CHRP), but that was what a lot of people thought the 1991 agreement was all about. The bottom line is that you shouldn't expect to see anything in the way of a 'compatible' PowerPC – apart from some pretty fast Mac derivatives – before the end of the century.

Portable PCs

Portable PCs have for a number of years been on the 'next big thing' list, but have never really looked like taking over from the desktop PC. The main reason for this is the expense of portable PCs and the fact that they are fiendishly difficult to upgrade – say as new and better technology becomes available. In general portable PCs are less useful than their desktop brethren since they have fewer expansion possibilities, with the added disincentive that virtually all peripherals, add-ons and accessories are far more expensive. Screen resolutions also tend to be inferior, being limited to VGA (640x480) – although some portables allow you to scroll around a larger virtual screen.

Over the years, three types of portable PC have appeared, the 'clam shell' or lap-top computer, the 'lunch-box' and the transportable PC. The lap-top has evolved into the notebook PC which is the most compact of all the IBM PC family.

Due to physical constraints, ISA type expansion cards cannot be used with notebook PCs, but most current models can use expansion cards based on the PCI bus. Although there are a few music based PCI cards – for instance the Roland SCP-55 SoundCanvas – there is nowhere near the diversity of cards as for desktop ISA PCs. One

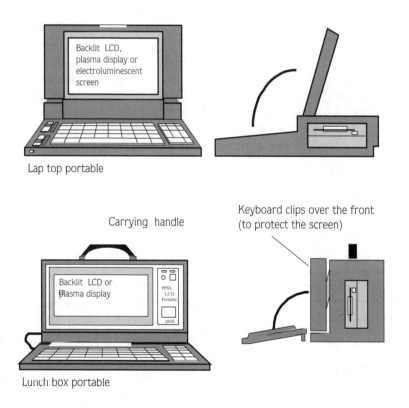

Lap top portable

Lunch box portable

Figure 8.1 The lap top and lunch box PCs

solution to this problem is the 'docking station' which has all the bits of a desktop PC that have been left out of the notebook due to lack of space. Docking stations are usually specific to a particular model of notebook PC, and it may well be cheaper to buy a moderately priced desktop PC.

The big advantage of a Notebook PC is its portability, and the producer on the move or the touring live musician can take the facilities of their computer based studio on the road. One crucial point to consider when purchasing a portable PC is how long the batteries will last, which can vary a lot between different models. Other important aspects to consider are the type of PCI cards that can be supported – there are three variants – and whether you need a built in CD-ROM. Remember the more add-ons you have, the shorter the battery life will be.

If you need a portable PC but don't need the option of running off batteries then the 'lunch box' configuration is worth looking at. These usually have expansion facilities for two or three ISA cards, which means that they are an ideal platform for a transportable PC based music system. For instance Studio Audio and Video Ltd do a portable version of their SADiE hard disk recording system based on just this configuration. Both this type of portable and the notebooks mentioned above usually have the ability to drive an external monitor at VGA or higher resolution which means you can use a big screen in you normal working environment, just relying on the built in screen when you are on the road.

The light fantastic

Over the short history of the PC the graphics facilities have improved considerably. The original PC had the choice of a text based monochrome display (MDA) or a colour display adapter (CGA) which gave fairly coarse resolution. Almost immediately the Hercules Graphics Adapter (HGA) high resolution monochrome expansion card was produced showing one of the advantages of the IBM design, expandability. If you don't like part of the design then you can improve on it by buying an appropriate 'add on' card. CGA evolved into EGA (enhanced graphics adapter) and then the VGA (video graphics array) to give higher resolutions and improved colour graphics.

The current *de facto* standard is Super VGA which is really a delineation of available resolutions rather than a hard and fast technical specification. The almost universal take up of Windows – with its device independence – has meant that the actual hardware details of a display adapter are less important than they used to be, since each video card is supplied with a display driver for Windows.

The resolution of a computer screen is usually specified in terms of the number of individually addressable dots on the screen which are called pixels (short for picture elements). So a CGA screen has a resolution of 640 dots across the screen by 200 dots from the top to the bottom, this is usually referred to as a 640 x 200 graphic resolution. The Hercules graphic adapter on the other hand has a 720 x 348 resolution though only in monochrome. The more recent the adapter, the higher the resolution, so the EGA gave 640 x 350 and the VGA 640 x 480 pixels or dots per screen. The three most common Super VGA resolutions are 800 x 600, 1024 x 768 and 1280 x 1024, though you really need to have a large monitor (say 17 inches) to take advantage of the last two.

The other important specification of a video system is its colour resolution – or the number of colours it can display. To be able to display any colour, a video card needs to be able to display '24 bit' colour. This means that the red, green and blue (RGB) elements for any particular pixel are be encoded as eight bit values – this is called 'True Colour' – and gives the best results. To achieve this the video card must store three bytes of information for each pixel on the screen, so for a standard VGA screen (640x480) the card would need to have at least 921,600 bytes of RAM on it while a 1280x1024 resolution screen would need just under 8 megabytes of RAM.

To get around this storage requirement an alternative method of colour encoding is used which has a fixed table of colour values – called a palette – that determines the colour of each pixel. So for instance to palettise an image with a 256 (or 8 bit) colour resolution, a table of colour values (256 colours x 3 byte colour information = 768 bytes) and a one byte index into this data structure for each pixel on the screen must be allocated. Thus for a VGA screen (640x480 = 307,200 bytes) the video card RAM requirement is reduced to 307,986 bytes, or around a third of the true colour equivalent. Reducing the number of colours to 16 (or 4 bit colour) gives even greater savings as two palette indexes can be packed into a single byte, meaning that the colour indexes of two pixels can be defined by each byte of video RAM.

The palette method can give good results, with 8-bit colour giving almost photographic quality, mainly due to the fact that most images use only a fairly limited range of colours. The problem with eight bit colour occurs when more than one image is displayed on the screen at the same time. As any two images are unlikely to use the same choice of colours (or palette) only one image will display properly since a video card can only load one palette at a time. The other image will suffer from palette shift distortion as the image is displayed with the indexes 'pointing' at the wrong colours, which can give some very odd – and not particularly useful – video effects. The need for palettising the screen is becoming less common as video technology improves, but is worth being aware of the effects – especially if you are planning to do any multimedia development.

Choosing a PC

This leaves you with a bewildering set of choices to make to select the computer system that is right for you. There are three questions you must ask yourself in deciding which computer to buy:

- How much computing power do I need?
- What kind of graphics do I require?
- Does the PC need to be portable?

The answer to the first question will depend on the type of music application that you wish to perform. So for instance, an entry level 486/SX will be adequate for most Windows based MIDI sequencing systems though a 386 or even an old 286 AT will be adequate if you use DOS based software. On the other hand, if you are going to use your PC as an MPC-based hard-disk recording system then you should go for the most powerful PC you can afford. The addition of a graphical user interface such as Microsoft's Windows places quite a heavy strain on the system which can be relieved to a certain extent by getting a graphics accelerator video card.

Hardware add-ons

As we have stressed throughout the book the PC's strongest point is its acceptance of expansion cards to give the computer extra facilities. We have mentioned several possibilities in previous chapters in the MIDI, DSP and SMPTE/EBU interface cards. There are various other types of expansion cards available, from tape interfaces and other peripheral memory storage devices to various types of controller for capturing analogue signals and user input. To a certain extent your additional hardware will depend on the use you plan to put your PC to; for instance if you're putting together a hard disk recording system you may want a tape drive for backing up your work, or if you are producing music scores then a high quality printer should be on your shopping list. Expansion cards for interfacing to the telephone network are quite handy as well, either FAX cards, modem cards or even voice input – that can turn your computer into an intelligent answering machine.

Of mice and modems

The two most common external devices that you can attach to your PC are the mouse and the modem. The mouse is probably the most common 'pointing' device used in the Windows, Icons, Mouse, Pointer (WIMP) style of interface popularised by the Apple Macintosh and available on the PC using Microsoft's Windows environment. Most PCs come supplied with a mouse, but some don't so it is worth checking before you buy. The modem is a device that allows your PC to communicate electronically with other computers using the Public Switched Telephone Network (PSTN). For more details on this topic see Appendix B.

There are various 'breeds' of mice, they can either connect to a spare serial port (a serial mouse) or connect to a special expansion card (a BUS mouse). The standard rodent detects movement from a rubber ball which rotates as you move the mouse, whereas some mice detect movement by reflecting light off a grid (an optical mouse). The type of mouse you use rather depends on your personal preference, but you need to have a spare serial port for a serial mouse or a spare expansion slot for a bus mouse. There are other possibilities, one of the authors uses tracker balls for the computer systems in his studio, owing to the small footprint and extra control they give. Other alternatives are touch screens and remote control devices that allow you to control the mouse pointer from across the room, which could be very useful in the recording environment.

Modems come in various flavours as well, but the differences between them are more fundamental and important. The word modem incidentally, is short for MOdulator/DEModulator, which describes the method by which the electronic signal is converted into an audio signal (modulated) so that it can be transmitted over a standard telephone line, and then converted back again (demodulated) at the other end. This technique is very similar to that used to synchronise the computer to a tape machine except that here the information is computer data rather than timing information.

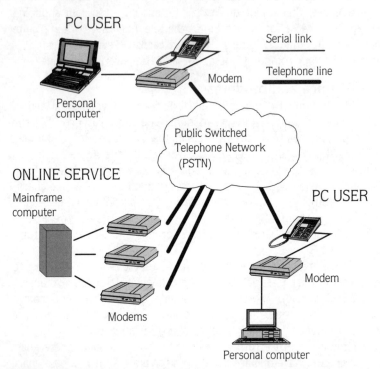

Figure 8.2 Using a modem to communicate electronically with other users and commercial 'on-line' services using the telephone network (PSTN)

There are two important features of a modem, the first is the speed at which it will operate, and the second is how compatible it is to other modems. The maximum speed at which a modem operates will define both how useful it is, and to a great extent, its price. The current entry level for modems is the V.34bis standard (14,400), usually with a FAX modem capability. The higher the speed of your modem the lower the running cost by reducing both the call charges and the time the computer is tied up with the data transfer. The compatibility factor will define whether the audio signal put out by the modem will be understood by the modem at the other end of the telephone line. Most on-line systems and fast modems will be able to connect to older, slower types, which means that if you can get your hands on a older modem – which have virtually no resale value – you will still be able to use it, though only within the constraints of its performance.

The different types of modem are:

Standard	Speed (baud)	Speed chars/sec*	Comments
V.21	300	30	Slowest, cheapest and obsolete
V.23	1200/75	120/7.5	As used by Prestel
V.22**	1200	120	
V.22bis	2400	240	Prone to line noise
V.32	9600	960	Must have error correction
V.32bis	14,400	1,440	Usually have fax capability
V.34	28,800	2,880	Usually have fax capability

Notes:
* This is without any form of data compression
** V.42 and V.42bis are error correction and compression protocols and can be used in conjunction with any of the above, though usually only on V.22 and above.

All modern modems have error correction, which usually complies with the V.42 international standard. To see why this is necessary, imagine that you are speaking to someone on the telephone. If there is noise on the line you can usually get the gist of the conversation, computers on the other hand, need to have a noise or error free line. This is achieved by having an error correcting line protocol, which means that if some of the data being transferred becomes garbled, the receiving computer will ask the sender to repeat the portion of data that was lost. The international standard for error correction is called V.42 which is a super-set of the *de facto* industry standard called MNP (Microcom Networking Protocol). The error correction is usually performed by the modem rather than the computers, thus taking the processing load away from the computer. We discuss a few of the services that you can access via a modem in Appendix B.

Upgrading the system

One of the great things about the PC is that if you have out-grown a particular machine, you can upgrade to a more powerful computer without having to repurchase all your software or learn how to use a new operating system. Furthermore you will be probably be able to install your old expansion cards into the new machine, giving you immediate access to all the facilities you had on your older, less powerful machine. Of course, you won't always have to move to a new machine, if you just need improved graphics then all you need to purchase is a new graphics adapter and monitor, if you need more speed then there are accelerator cards that will improve the performance.

Another way of upgrading a PC is to replace its processor with a faster variant. Some recent 486 motherboards have an Intel Overdrive socket which allows the replacement of the 80486 processor with a cut-down version of the Pentium chip. Another alternative is to replace the 486 with a double or triple clocked version of the chip which can improve performance considerably. You will need to check the PC documentation to see if either of these options are available on your machine.

Software environments

One of the traditional criticisms of the PC has been the apparent 'unfriendliness' of the MS/DOS operating system. The Apple Macintosh has always been supplied with a WIMP style user interface, making it easier for a novice to use. But at what cost? The early Macintosh's were painfully slow and had comparatively little memory for the running of user programs. The advantage of the MS/DOS operating system is that it takes up a relatively small amount of the PC's system resources allowing the computer to run at nearly its maximum speed.

However the introduction of Windows 3.0 and later variants has more or less scotched that particular complaint, and the introduction of Windows 95 in the second half of 1995 was the most successful launch of an operating system ever. Unlike Windows 3.x which ran in conjunction with MS-DOS, Windows 95 is a completely integrated operating system which can run 32 bit applications, though parts of the operating system are still based on 16 bit code. Windows 95 is a full blown multi-tasking system that allows you to run a number of programs simultaneously. For situations where Windows is inappropriate for some reason, there are also several non-graphically oriented user interfaces available for the PC, from simple menu systems like Executive Systems' XTREE program to Quarterdeck's DESQview which, like Windows, has full multi-tasking facilities.

Multi-user and multi-tasking systems

Traditionally, one of the main reasons for going for a powerful computer is to be able to run more than one program at a time, (multi-tasking) or to let a number of people use the same computer simultaneously (multi-user). Both these cases involve the computer running more than one program at the same time. These two attributes are not mutually exclusive, for instance UNIX is a multi-user, multi-tasking operating system, i.e. that more than one person can use the computer at the same time and each person can run more than one program. Windows, on the other hand, is just a multi-tasking system, so it can be used only by one person, but they can run more than one program. Multi-user systems are a good way of getting the most out of an expensive but powerful computer by making the power available to a large number of people. Multi-tasking is a way of improving the computer user's productivity, since the computer could be used for some keyboard intensive task (like word processing) which doesn't require much of the computer's processing power, whilst also performing some heavy processing task (like a database search) which would otherwise tie up the computer for a long period.

Earlier on in the book we mentioned the principle that There Ain't No Such Thing As A Free Lunch. Well, this applies here as well. A central processing unit (CPU), which is the heart of the computer, can run only one program at a time. So what a multi-whatever operating system does is divide the computer's processing unit equally between the users and/or tasks that it has to perform. This is usually done on a time basis, the operating system will load a program, run it for a few milliseconds and then go on to the next program. In this way, each program will get a chance to be run, albeit more slowly than it would on a single user/task system. The apparent performance of an individual program would be degraded in proportion to the number of other programs and the overhead of the operating system, as it swaps between programs.

When we consider the requirements of a music system we can see the disadvantages of this for some music applications. If we want to run a sequencing program then it is important that the incoming MIDI data is accurately time-stamped so that it can be replayed with fidelity. On a multi-tasking system this is difficult to do reliably, since the CPU may be running another program at the time the MIDI data arrives. From the musician's point of view this would show up as timing errors or even lost note events, a situation which is obviously not desirable.

These problems can be solved by adding complexity to the operating system or the interface hardware which in turn will increase the cost of the computer system and probably make the whole thing less reliable. On the other hand, for applications such as scoring, where you are not dealing with real-time music input, multi-tasking could be a real boon as you could print out one score whilst working on another. Since printing a score is a time consuming activity which would normally tie up the computer for long periods, the small reduction in performance would be offset by an increase in your personal productivity.

The two most common multi-tasking systems for the PC are Microsoft's Windows, which is also a GUI (or WIMP system) and QuarterDeck's DESQview which isn't. Windows is actually a 'family' of operating system products aimed at different working environments, with Windows 3.x and Windows 95 aimed at the small office and home user, while Windows NT is aimed at the corporate user. IBM's OS/2 and Warp products are also being pushed heavily at the time of writing but don't seem to be making much headway against the global dominance of Windows. Two other current operating systems for the PC hardware platform are the various versions of AT&T's UNIX and the low cost clone 'Linux', though these have virtually no support for music applications.

The future
The future of the PC still looks to be pretty assured at the time of writing, with Intel bringing out more powerful processors and Microsoft pushing back the boundaries of the MS/DOS derived operating systems with the introduction of Windows 95, and don't forget that Windows NT is waiting in the wings. With the failure of the PowerPC to make any significant impact on the computing market and Apple's persistence in keeping i's 'closed' architecture there doesn't seem to

be any credible contender for the PC's role of being a computer for the masses. In short, the PC looks like it's going to be around for a some time yet.

On the software front, applications like multimedia – which brings together high quality graphics, speech and music technology to be used in corporate as well as entertainment fields – will ensure that the PC will live on as a software platform. The corporate multimedia market could also provide a new outlet for original compositions from the computer-based musician.

System set-ups

The sort of PC MIDI system you need depends rather on what you intend to do with your music. If you just want to tinker with computer music on your PC to get the feel for what's possible then all you need is a MIDI card, a low cost sequencer package and some form of sound generator.

The most usual sound generator is some form of electronic synthesiser or organ, most modern instruments have MIDI ports as standard equipment. If you're actively interested in music, then you probably already have something suitable. And you're not necessarily tied to the organ or piano style keyboard, if you don't play keyboards and don't care to learn, then there are alternatives such as the Casio Horn or Yamaha WX11 for wind players, the Roland or Yamaha guitar controllers or even the Hohner MIDI accordions.

You can even build your own controller, one the authors has built a MIDI controller based on the free reed instrument called the Melodeon.

The best places to look for MIDI instruments are in magazines like *Sound on Sound* or the *Computer Music Journal.*

Personal computer workstation

System requirements
Computer: 486SX/25 (or better) with 4 MB of RAM
PC/interface: Roland SCC-1 card (or similar)
Software: Windows 3.x, Cakewalk Home Studio or Cubasis
Peripherals: Mouse, printer (optional)
Instruments: MIDI capable keyboard (e.g. Roland PC-2000 or Yamaha CBX-K3)

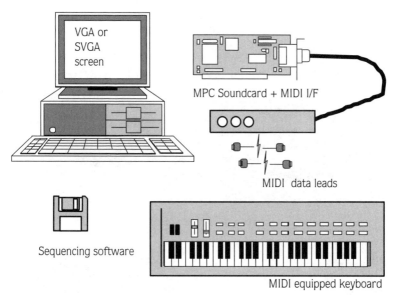

Figure 9.1 The PC music workstation

Scoring systems

System requirements
Computer: 486DX/33 (or better) with 8 MB of RAM
PC/interface: Any MPU-401 compatible
Software: Windows 3.x or Windows 95, MusicTime or
MusicProse
Peripherals: Mouse, graphic printer (e.g. HP DeskJet)
Instruments: MIDI capable keyboard (optional)

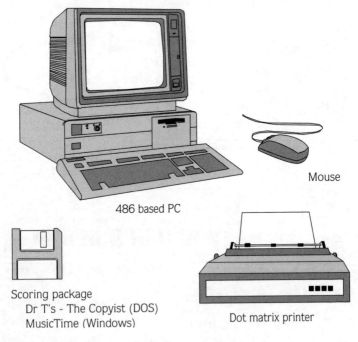

Mouse

486 based PC

Scoring package
Dr T's - The Copyist (DOS)
MusicTime (Windows)

Dot matrix printer

Figure 9.2(a) The low cost PC music notation system

System requirements:
Computer: 486DX4 or Pentium PC
PC/interface: MPU-401 compatible or MPC Soundcard
Software: Windows 95, Finale
Peripherals: Mouse, laser printer (e.g. HP LaserJet), Postscript
(optional)
Instruments: MIDI capable keyboard (optional)

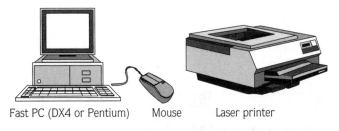

Fast PC (DX4 or Pentium) Mouse Laser printer

Scoring package:
Score (DOS)
Finale (Windows)

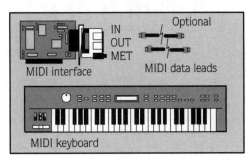

Figure 9.2(b) The professional PC music notation (desk top publishing)
system

The PC as a backing band

System requirements
Computer: Notebook PC
PC/interface: Roland SCP-55 with MCB-3 MIDI connector
(optional)
Software: Cakewalk Professional or Cubase
Peripherals: Mouse (optional)
Instruments: MIDI capable keyboard and expander module(s)
(e.g. SoundCanvas) or sound module with serial interface (e.g.
Yamaha MU80)

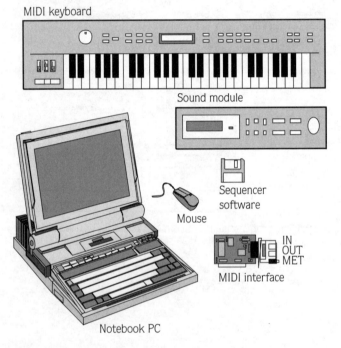

Figure 9.3 The portable PC set-up for use in live performance

The tapeless MIDI home studio

System requirements
Computer: 486SX/25 with 4 MB of RAM
PC/interface: Any Windows compatible MIDI interface
Software: Cakewalk Professional or Cubase Score
Peripherals: Mouse, printer (optional)
Instruments: MIDI capable keyboard
Expander module(s) (e.g. Roland D110, SoundCanvas)
Stereo mixing desk
Digital effects units (e.g. Alesis QuadraVerb)

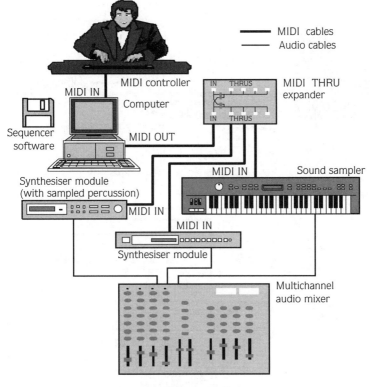

Figure 9.4(a) The tapeless MIDI studio

The guitarist's MIDI home studio

System requirements
Computer: 486SX/25 with 4 MB of RAM
PC/interface: Windows compatible MIDI interface/soundcard
G-Vox PC guitar system (connects to serial port)
Software: PowerChords (from Howling Dog Systems)
Peripherals: Mouse, printer (optional)
Instruments: Guitar (acoustic or electric)
MIDI capable keyboard (optional)
Expander module(s) (e.g. Roland D110, SoundCanvas)
Stereo mixing desk and digital effects units

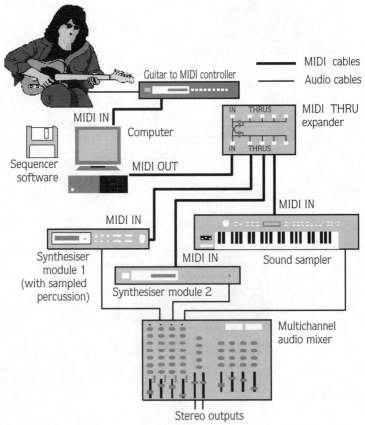

Figure 9.4(b) The guitar based MIDI studio

The multitrack/MIDI studio

System requirements
Computer: 486SX/25 with 4 MB of RAM
PC/interface: MIDI Interface with SMPTE input/output
Software: Cakewalk Professional or Cubase Score
Peripherals: Mouse, printer (optional)
Instruments: MIDI capable keyboard
Expander module(s) (e.g. Roland D110)
MIDI controlled digital effects (e.g. MIDIVerb)
Multi-channel mixing desk
Multi-track tape recorder (or portastudio)

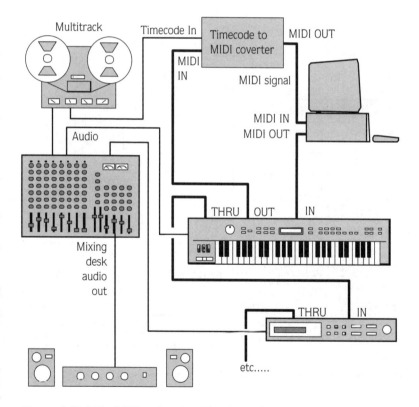

Figure 9.5(a) The MIDI equipped multitrack tape studio

The digital multitrack/MIDI studio

System requirements
Computer: 486SX/25 with 4 MB of RAM
PC/interface: Any Windows compatible MIDI interface
Software: Cakewalk Professional or Cubase Score
Peripherals: Mouse, printer (optional)
Instruments: MIDI capable keyboard
Expander module(s) (e.g. Roland D110)
MIDI controlled digital effects (e.g. MIDIVerb)
Multi-channel mixing desk
Alesis ADAT
JL Cooper DATASync2 or Steinberg ACI

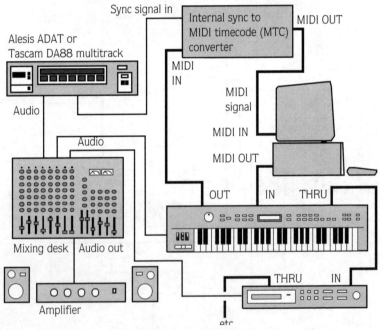

Figure 9.5(b) The MIDI equipped multitrack tape studio

Budget MPC digital audio workstation

System requirements
Computer: 486DX4/100 or Pentium with at least 8 MB of RAM
PC/interface: Gravis UltraSound Max or SoundBlaster type soundcard
Software: Cubasis Audio
Peripherals: Mouse, large capacity hard disk drive
Instruments: Acoustic and MIDI instruments

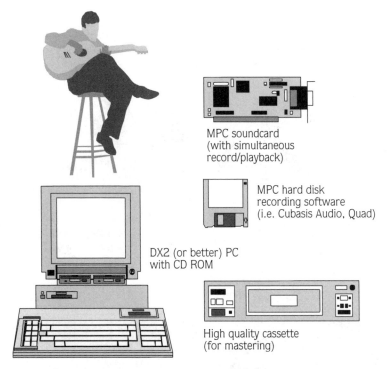

MPC soundcard
(with simultaneous
record/playback)

MPC hard disk
recording software
(i.e. Cubasis Audio, Quad)

DX2 (or better) PC
with CD ROM

High quality cassette
(for mastering)

Figure 9.6(a) Budget MPC digital audio workstation

MPC digital audio workstation

System requirements
Computer: 486DX4/100 or Pentium with at least 8 MB of RAM
PC/interface: Turtle Beach Tahiti, Monterey or Tropez or DAL
CardD, or Roland RAP-10
Software: Software Audio Workshop or Samplitude with
Cubase or Cakewalk, or Cakewalk Audio, Cubase Audio
Peripherals: Mouse, large capacity hard disk drive
Instruments: Acoustic and MIDI instruments

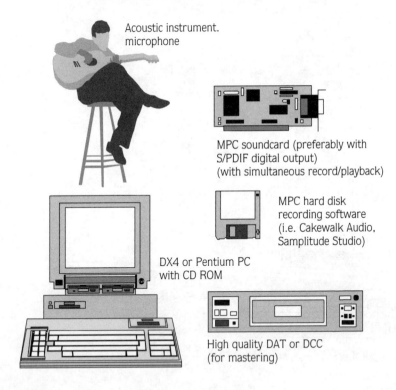

Acoustic instrument.
microphone

MPC soundcard (preferably with
S/PDIF digital output)
(with simultaneous record/playback)

MPC hard disk
recording software
(i.e. Cakewalk Audio,
Samplitude Studio)

DX4 or Pentium PC
with CD ROM

High quality DAT or DCC
(for mastering)

Figure 9.6(b) The MPC digital audio workstation

Professional digital audio workstation

System requirements
Computer: 486DX/33 or Pentium with at least 8 MB of RAM
PC/interface: SoundScape SSHDR-1 or Digidesign Session-8
or Studio Audio and Video SADiE (choice will depend on
application)
Software: Supplied with system
Peripherals: Mouse
Large capacity hard disk drive(s) (friendly bank manager)
Instruments: Acoustic

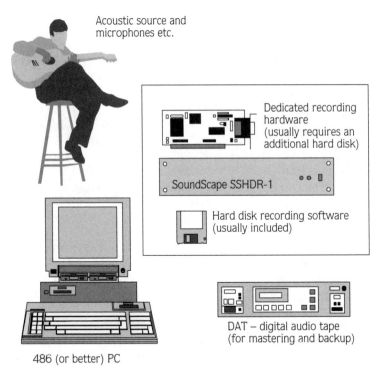

Acoustic source and
microphones etc.

Dedicated recording
hardware
(usually requires an
additional hard disk)

SoundScape SSHDR-1

Hard disk recording software
(usually included)

DAT – digital audio tape
(for mastering and backup)

486 (or better) PC

Figure 9.7 Professional direct-to-disk recording system based on the PC

Appendix A
The MIDI Specification 1.0

Introduction

MIDI is the acronym for Musical Instrument Digital Interface. MIDI enables synthesisers, sequencers, home computers, rhythm machines, etc. to be interconnected through a standard interface.

Each MIDI-equipped instrument usually contains a receiver and a transmitter. Some instruments may contain only a receiver or transmitter. The receiver receives messages in MIDI format and executes MIDI commands. It consists of an opto-isolator, universal asynchronous receiver/transmitter (UART), and other hardware needed to perform the intended functions. The transmitter originates messages in MIDI format, and transmits them by way of a UART and line driver.

The MIDI standard hardware and data format are defined in this specification.

Conventions

Status and data bytes given in Tables I through VI are given in binary. Numbers followed by an H are in hexadecimal. All other numbers are in decimal.

Hardware

The interface operates at 31.25 (+/- 1%) kbaud, asynchronous, with a start bit, 8 data bits (D0 to D7), and a stop bit. This makes a total of 10 bits for a period of 320 microseconds per serial byte.

Circuit: 5 mA current loop type. Logical 0 is current ON. One output shall drive one and only one input. The receiver shall be opto-isolated and require less than 5 mA to turn on. Sharp PC-900 and HP

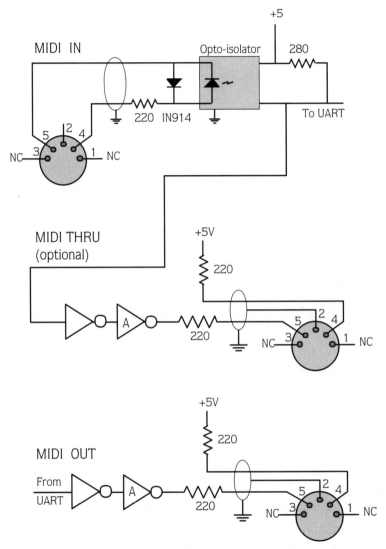

Figure A.1 MIDI standard hardware
1 Suitable opto isolators are Sharp PC-900 or HP 6N138 (with appropriate changes)
2 Gates A are IC or transistor
3 Resistor values are in ohms and are 5% tolerance

6N138 opto-isolators have been found acceptable. Other high-speed opto-isolators may be satisfactory. Rise and fall times should be less than 2 microseconds.

Connectors: DIN 5 pin (180 degree) female panel mount receptacle. An example is the Switchcraft 57 GB5F. The connectors shall be labelled 'MIDI IN' and 'MIDI OUT'. Note that pins 1 and 3 are not used, and should be left unconnected in the receiver and transmitter.

Cables shall have a maximum length of 50 feet (15 metres), and shall be terminated on each end by a corresponding 5-pin DIN male plug, such as the Switchcraft 05GM5M. The cable shall be shielded twisted pair, with the shield connected to pin 2 at both ends.

A 'MIDI THRU' output may be provided if needed, which provides a direct copy of data coming in MIDI IN. For very long chain lengths (more than three instruments), higher-speed opto-isolators must be used to avoid additive rise/fall time errors which affect pulse width duty cycle.

Data format

All MIDI communication is achieved through multi-byte 'messages' consisting of one status byte followed by one or two data bytes, except real-time and exclusive messages (see below).

Message types

Messages are divided into two main categories: channel and system.

Channel

Channel messages contain a four-bit number in the status byte which address the message specifically to one of 16 channels. These messages are thereby intended for any units in a system whose channel number matches the channel number encoded into the status byte.

There are two types of channel messages: voice and mode.

Voice

To control the instrument's voices, voice messages are sent over the voice channels.

Mode

To define the instrument's response to voice messages, mode messages are sent over the instrument's basic channel.

System

System messages are not encoded with channel numbers. There are three types of system messages: common, real-time, and exclusive.

Common

Common messages are intended for all units in a system.

Real-time

Real-time messages are intended for all units in a system. They contain status bytes only – no data bytes. Real-time messages may be sent at any time – even between bytes of a message which has a different status. In such cases the real-time message is either ignored or acted upon, after which the receiving process resumes under the previous status.

Exclusive

Exclusive messages can contain any number of data bytes, and are terminated by an end of exclusive (EOX) or any other status byte. These messages include a manufacturer's identification (ID) code. If the receiver does not recognise the ID code, it should ignore the ensuing data. So that other users can fully access MIDI instruments, manufacturers should publish the format of data following their ID code. Only the manufacturer can update the format following their ID.

Data types

Status bytes

Status bytes are eight-bit binary numbers in which the most significant bit (MSB) is set (binary 1). Status bytes serve to identify the message type, that is, the purpose of the data bytes which follow the status byte.

Except for real-time messages, new status bytes will always command the receiver to adopt their status, even if the new status is received before the last message was completed

Running status

For voice and mode messages only, when a status byte is received and processed, the receiver will remain in that status until a different status byte is received. Therefore, if the same status byte would be repeated, it may (optionally) be omitted so that only the correct number of data bytes need be sent. Under running status, then, a complete message need only consist of specified data bytes sent in the specified order. The running status feature is especially useful for communicating long strings of note on/off messages, where 'note on with velocity of 0' is used for note off. (A separate note off status byte is also available.)

Running status will be stopped when any other status byte intervenes, except that real-time messages will only interrupt the running status temporarily.

Unimplemented status

Any status bytes received for functions which the receiver has not implemented should be ignored, and subsequent data bytes ignored.

Undefined status

Undefined status bytes must not be used. Care should be taken to prevent illegal messages from being sent during power-up or power-down. If undefined status bytes are received, they should be ignored, as should subsequent data bytes.

Data bytes

Following the status byte, there are (except for real-time messages) one or two data bytes which carry the content of the message. Data bytes are eight-bit binary numbers in which the MSB is reset (binary 0). The number and range of data bytes which must follow each status byte are specified in the tables which follow. For each status byte the correct number of data bytes must always be sent. Inside the receiver, action on the message should wait until all data bytes required under the current status are received. Receivers should ignore data bytes which have not been properly preceded by a valid status byte (with the exception of 'running status,' above).

Channel modes

Synthesisers contain sound generation elements called voices. Voice assignment is the algorithmic process of routing note on/off data from the keyboard to the voices so that the musical notes are correctly played with accurate timing.

When MIDI is implemented, the relationship between the 16 available MIDI channels and the synthesiser's voice assignment must be defined. Several mode messages are available for this purpose (see Table III). They are omni (on/off), poly, and mono. Poly and mono are mutually exclusive, i.e. poly select disables mono, and vice versa. Omni, when on, enables the receiver to receive voice messages in all voice channels without discrimination. When omni is off, the receiver will accept voice messages from only the selected voice channel(s). Mono, when on, restricts the assignment of voices to just one voice per voice channel (monophonic.) When mono is off (= poly on), any number of voices may be allocated by the receiver's normal voice assignment algorithm (polyphonic.)

For a receiver assigned to basic channel 'N,' the four possible modes arising from the two mode messages are:

mode	omni		
1	on	poly	voice messages are received from all voice channels and assigned to voices polyphonically
2	on	mono	voice messages are received from all voice channels, and control only one voice, monophonically
3	off	poly	voice messages are received in voice channel N only, and are assigned to voices polyphonically
4	off	mono	voice messages are received in voice channels N thru N+M-1, and assigned monophonically to voices 1 thru M, respectively. The number of voices M is specified by the third byte of the mono mode message

Four modes are applied to transmitters (also assigned to basic channel N). Transmitters with no channel selection capability will normally transmit on basic channel 1 (N=0).

mode	omni		
1	on	poly	all voice messages are transmitted in channel N
2	on	mono	voice messages for one voice are sent in channel N
3	off	poly	voice messages for all voices are sent in channel N
4	off	mono	voice messages for voices 1 thru M are transmitted in voice channels N thru N+M-1, respectively (single voice per channel)

A MIDI receiver or transmitter can operate under one and only one mode at a time. Usually the receiver and transmitter will be in the same mode. If a mode cannot be honoured by the receiver, it may ignore the message (and any subsequent data bytes), or it may switch to an alternate mode (usually mode 1, omni on/poly).

Mode messages will be recognised by a receiver only when sent in the Basic channel to which the receiver has been assigned, regardless of the current mode. Voice messages may be received in the Basic channel and in other channels (which are all called voice channels), which are related specifically to the Basic channel by the rules above, depending on which mode has been selected.

A MIDI receiver may be assigned to one or more Basic channels by default or by user control. For example, an eight-voice synthesiser might be assigned to Basic channel 1 on power-up. The user could then switch the instrument to be configured as two four-voice synthesisers, each assigned to its own Basic channel. Separate mode messages would then be sent to each four-voice synthesiser, just as if they were physically separate instruments.

Power-up default conditions

On power-up all instruments should default to mode #1. Except for note on/off status, all voice messages should be disabled. Spurious or undefined transmissions must be suppressed.

Table I Summary of status bytes

Status D7–D0	# of data bytes	Description
Channel voice messages		
1000nnnn	2	note off event
1001nnnn	2	note on event (velocity=0: note off)
1010nnnn	2	polyphonic key pressure/after touch
1011nnnn	2	control change
1100nnnn	1	program change
1101nnnn	1	channel pressure/after touch
1110nnnn	2	pitch bend change

Channel mode messages

1011nnnn	2	selects channel mode

System messages

11110000	*****	system exclusive
11110sss	0 to 2	system common
11111ttt	0	system real time

Notes:
nnnn: N-1, where N = channel #,
i.e. 0000 is channel 1.
0001 is channel 2.

.

.

1111 is channel 16.

*****: Oiiiiiii, data, ..., EOX
iiiiiii: Identification
sss: 1 to 7
ttt: 0 to 7

Table II Channel voice messages

Status	Data bytes	Description
1000nnnn	0kkkkkkk	note off (see notes 1-4)
	0vvvvvvv	vvvvvvv: note off velocity
1001nnnn	0kkkkkkk	note on (see notes 1-4)
	0vvvvvvv	vvvvvvv – 0: velocity
		vvvvvvv = 0: note off
1010nnnn	0kkkkkkk	polyphonic key pressure (aftertouch)
	0vvvvvvv	vvvvvvv: pressure value
1011nnnn	0ccccccc	control change
	0vvvvvvv	ccccccc: control # (0-121) (notes 5-8)
		vvvvvvv: control value

> cccccc = 122 thru 127: Reserved.
> (See Table III)
>
> 1100nnnn Oppppppp program change
>   ppppppp: program number (0-127)
> 1101nnnn Ovvvvvv   channel pressure (aftertouch)
>   vvvvvvv: pressure value
> 1110nnnn Ovvvvvv   pitch bend change LSB (see note 10)
>   Ovvvvvv   pitch bend change MSB

Notes:

1 nnnn: voice channel # (1-16, coded as defined in Table I notes)
2 kkkkkkk: note # (0 – 127)
   kkkkkkk = 60: middle C of keyboard

```
0  12  24  36  48  60  72  84  96  108 120 127
```

```
      c   c   c   c   c   c   c   c
      |———————— piano range ————————|
```

3 vvvvvvv: key velocity
   A logarithmic scale would be advisable.

```
0          1              64              127
```

```
off      ppp   pp   p   mp   mf   f   ff   fff
```

vvvvvvv = 64: in case of no velocity sensors
vvvvvvv = 0: note off, with velocity = 64

4 Any note on message sent should be balanced by sending a note
   off message for that note in that channel at some later time.
5 cccccc: control number

cccccc	Description
0	continuous controller 0 MSB
1	continuous controller 1 MSB (modulation bender)
2	continuous controller 2 MSB
3	continuous controller 3 MSB

4-31	continuous controllers 4-31 MSB
32	continuous controller 0 LSB
33	continuous controller 1 LSB (modulation bender)
34	continuous controller 2 LSB
35	continuous controller 3 LSB
36-63	continuous controllers 4-31 LSB
64-95	switches (on/off)
96-121	undefined
122-127	reserved for channel mode messages (see Table III)

6 All controllers are specifically defined by agreement of the MIDI Manufacturers' Association (MMA) and the Japan MIDI Standards Committee (JMSC). Manufacturers can request through the MMA or JMSC that logical controllers be assigned to physical ones as necessary. The controller allocation table must be provided in the user's operation manual.

7 Continuous controllers are divided into most significant and least significant bytes. If only seven bits of resolution are needed for any particular controllers, only the MSB is sent. It is not necessary to send the LSB. If more resolution is needed, then both are sent, first the MSB, then the LSB. If only the LSB has changed in value, the LSB may be sent without re-sending the MSB.

8 vvvvvvv: control value (MSB)

(for controllers)

```
 0                                                     127
|------------------------------------------------------|
 min                                                   max
```

(for switches)

```
 0                                                     127
|------------------------------------------------------|
 off                                                   on
```

Numbers 1 through 126, inclusive, are ignored.

9 Any messages (e.g. note on), which are sent successively under the same status, can be sent without a status byte until a different status byte is needed.

10 Sensitivity of the pitch bender is selected in the receiver. Centre position value (no pitch change) is 2000H, which would be transmitted EnH-OOH-40H.

Table III Channel mode messages

Status	Data bytes	Description
1011nnnn	Occccccc Ovvvvvv	Mode messages
		ccccccc = 122: local control
		vvvvvvv = 0, local control off
		vvvvvvv = 127, local control on
		ccccccc = 123: all notes off
		vvvvvv = 0
		ccccccc = 124: omni mode off (all notes off)
		vvvvvv = 0
		ccccccc = 125: omni mode on (all notes off)
		vvvvvv = 0
		ccccccc = 126: mono mode on (poly mode off) (all notes off)
		vvvvvvv = M, where M is the number of channels.
		vvvvvvv = 0, the number of channels equals the number of voices in the receiver.
		ccccccc = 127: poly mode on (mono mode off)
		vvvvvv = 0 (all notes off)

Notes:
1 nnnn: basic channel # (1-16, coded as defined in Table I)
2 messages 123 thru 127 function as 'all notes off' messages. They will turn off all voices controlled by the assigned basic channel. Except for message 123, all notes off, they should not be sent periodically, but only for a specific purpose. In no case should they be used in lieu of

note off commands to turn off notes which have been previously turned on. Therefore any all notes off command (123-127) may be ignored by receiver with no possibility of notes staying on, since any note on command must have a corresponding specific note off command.

3 Control change #122, local control, is optionally used to interrupt the internal control path between the keyboard, for example, and the sound-generating circuitry. If 0 (local off mesage) is received, the path is disconnected: the keyboard data goes only to MIDI and the sound-generating circuitry is controlled only by incoming MIDI data. If a 7FH (local on message) is received, normal operation is restored.

4 The third byte of 'mono' specifies the number of channels in which monophonic voice messages are to be sent. This number, 'M', is a number between 1 and 16. The channel(s) being used, then, will be the current basic channel (= N) thru N+M-1 up to a maximum of 16. If M = 0, this is a special case directing the receiver to assign all its voices, one per channel, from the basic channel N through 16.

Table IV System common messages

Status	Data bytes	Description
11110001	Onnndddd	MIDI timecode quarter frame message nnn: message type dddd: data value (nibble)
11110010		Song position pointer
	Ollllll	llllll: (least significant)
	Ohhhhhhh	hhhhhhh: (most significant)
11110011	Osssssss	Song select ssssss: song #
11110100		Undefined
11110101		Undefined
11110110	none	Tune request
11110111	none	EOX: 'end of system exclusive' flag

Notes:
1 See the MIDI timecode for an explanation of this and other MIDI timecode messages.

2 Song position pointer: is an internal register which holds the number of MIDI beats (1 beat = 6 MIDI clocks) since the start of the song. Normally it is set to 0 when the START switch is pressed, which starts sequence playback. It then increments with every sixth MIDI clock receipt, until STOP is pressed. If CONTINUE is pressed, it continues to increment. It can be arbitrarily preset (to a resolution of 1 beat) by the Song Position Pointer message.

3 Song select: Specifies which song or sequence is to be played upon receipt of a start (real-time) message.

4 Tune request: Used with analog synthesisers to request them to tune their oscillators.

5 EOX: Used as a flag to indicate the end of a system exclusive transmission (see Table VI).

Table V System real time messages

Status	Data bytes	Description
11111000		Timing clock
11111001		Undefined
11111010		Start
11111011		Continue
11111100		Stop
11111101		Undefined
11111110		Active sensing
11111111		System reset

Notes:

1 The system real time messages are for synchronising all of the system in real time.

2 The system real time messages can be sent at any time. Any messages which consist of two or more bytes may be split to insert real time messages.

3 Timing clock (F8H). The system is synchronised with this clock, which is sent at a rate of 24 clocks/quarter note.

4 Start (from the beginning of song) (FAH). This byte is immediately sent when the PLAY switch on the master (e.g. sequencer or rhythm unit) is pressed.

5 Continue (FBH).This is sent when the CONTINUE switch is hit. A sequence will continue at the time of the next clock.

6 Stop (FCH). This byte is immediately sent when the STOP switch is hit. It will stop the sequence.

7 Active sensing (FEH). Use of this message is optional, for either receivers or transmitters. This is a 'dummy' status byte that is sent every 300 ms (max), whenever there is no other activity on MIDI. The receiver will operate normally if it never receives FEH. Otherwise, if FEH is ever received, the receiver will expect to receive FEH or a transmission of any type every 300 ms (max). If a period of 300 ms passes with no activity, the receiver will turn off the voices and return to normal operation.

8 System reset (FFH). This message initialises all of the system to the condition of just having turned on power. The system Reset message should be used sparingly, preferably under manual command only. In particular, it should not be sent automatically on power up.

Table VI System exclusive messages

Status	Data bytes	Description
11110000		Bulk dump etc.
	0iiiiiii	iiiiii: identification
	.	
	(0*******)	
	.	Any number of bytes may be sent
	.	here, for any purpose, as long
	.	as they all have a zero in the
	.	most significant bit.
	(0*******)	
	.	
11110111		EOX: 'End of system exclusive'

Notes:
1 iiiiii: identification ID (0-127)
2 All bytes between the system exclusive status byte and EOX or the next status byte must have zeroes in the MSB.
3 The ID number can be obtained from the MMA or JMSC.

4 In no case should other status or data bytes (except real-time) be interleaved with system exclusive, regardless of whether or not the ID code is recognised.

5 EOX or any other status byte, except real-time, will terminate a system exclusive message, and should be sent immediately at its conclusion.

Appendix B
On-line communications

Tapping into cyberspace

By its very nature, the creative work you do in your studio (or back bedroom) is solitary, or at least involves a very small number of people. This leads to two things, a sense of isolation and (possibly) the musical equivalent of writer's block due to lack of external influences. There are ways around these problems, for instance you can keep in touch by reading any of the excellent range of music magazines that appear on your newsagent's shelves every month. You can put a card up in your local music shop, ask everyone you meet if they have an interest in music, organise jams or even busk on the underground. All these things take up valuable time, and if you have to work (or study) for a living, then it doesn't leave much time for the main event. That is of course, making music.

Going on-line

One solution to the problems of keeping in touch is to go 'on-line'. For this, all you need is a computer, a modem and a telephone line. By paying as little as a hundred pounds for a modem and getting hold of some terminal software you can connect to a number of computer services based in the UK or overseas. Although this might seem to be a rather impersonal form of communication, there are certain advantages. It allows you to rub electronic shoulders with people all over the country (or even the world) that you couldn't hope to meet any other way. I have had electronic chin-wags with people I would have been very unlikely to have met otherwise.

In short, a computer and modem is a great leveller – you can swap tips with international stars, make suggestions to the writer of your favourite sequencer package and generally keep in touch without leaving the comfort of your music work-station. There are also tangible advantages as well – you can get synthesiser patches, sequences, free programs and software updates.

Incidentally, a modem (MOdulator/DEModulator) is just a little box that converts 'computer speak' from the serial port of your computer into an audio signal (i.e. modulation). This audio signal can then be sent down a telephone circuit and converted back into 'computer speak' at the other end (using another modem).

What's available

There are a number of multi-user systems based in the UK and the original (and best for musicians) system which is based in the USA. This appendix looks at the Performing Artists Network (PAN) and Compulink Information eXchange (CIX) (as we have had a lot of experience with these two systems) and the World Wide Web, which is a more general purpose way of networking. This is in no way meant to be a comprehensive look at what is available either world wide (or even in Europe), just a glance at a few systems. The first of these systems is aimed specifically at musicians and people involved in the music business, not only musicians but also people involved with record companies and the like. On the other hand, CIX is a public conferencing system which happens to have an active music technology section and a number of music industry people as users, there are also quite a number of participants who are interested in things musical.

PAN The Performing Artists Network

This is the original and best of all the music networks. Set up about ten years ago, it has several thousand members. Amongst the members are companies like Voyetra, Opcode, Digidesign and Apple Corporation. Originally, The PAN Network was known officially as 'The Performing Artists Network of North America', and was founded in 1981 as a self-help organisation for self-managed performers. Over the years, it has grown horizontally to include the entire entertainment industry and hence the management shortened the name to simply 'The PAN Network'. The guiding philosophy behind the network is that the industry is based on the discovery, development and 'packaging' of talent, and therefore, performing talent is the industry's most vital raw material. It is run by a musician (Perry Leopold), for musicians but also encompasses other elements of the music business such as equipment manufacturers, software developers and even lawyers who specialise in music business matters. It has a very strong North American bias, but has a number of regular international (mainly European) users.

```
Hello BRIANHEYWOOD

Welcome to The PAN Networks
Copyright (c) 1981-1995


Logon at   :  2-FEB-1996 09:24:58
Last Logon :  2-FEB-1996 06:03:25
<*> The PAN Network is pleased to announce FREE and UNLIMITED access to the
    World Wide Web for all PAN members.  Type GO US MEMBER!

MAIN>What do you want to do? ?


PAN Menu:

Audio-Net                Shopping
Availability System      Sigs & Usergroups
Business Networks        Support Hotlines
Classifieds              Synth & MIDI Networks
Conference               Travel Services
Internet Services        Workspace
PAN Mail                 Using PAN (Free)
Member Directory         HELP
News & Charts            EXIT

MAIN>What do you want to do?
```

Figure B.1 Opening screen of PAN, main menu

PAN is divided into two sections, one for the music business side and the other for the musicians and music software people. On the music side, PAN has a number of forums for general discussion of various subjects and Special Interest Groups (SIGs) covering different manufacturer's products. Each area also has a database from which you can download programs, patches, samples and other general interest material such as specifications and articles.

Since the American MIDI Manufacturers' Association uses PAN you can always get the most update to date version of the current MIDI specification. There is a lively discussion in progress about some aspect of the future of MIDI; this is very exciting since these are the people that can change the future of MIDI.

```
                          Welcome to PAN's
                   Synthesizer & MIDI Development Network
                   -----------------------------------------


SYNTH & MIDI>What do you want to do? ?


SYNTH & MIDI Menu:

Announcements          Poll
Classifieds            Shopping Service
Conference             Sigs & Usergroups
Databases              Support Hotline
PAN Mail               Synth & MIDI Newswire
Entry Log              Who's On
Forum (Messages)       Help
Member Directory       Exit

SYNTH & MIDI>What do you want to do?
```

Figure B.2 Performing Artists Network (PAN) Synth & MIDI area menu

```
General Interest       Sequencing
Patches                User Groups
MIDI Development       Guitar MIDI
Sampling               PC Applications
MAC Applications       Crossfire
Synth Maintenance      ST Applications
New & Noteworthy

TOPIC>Which topic? midi

DBASES:MID> (Dir, Read, Set, Exit)

Directory of All Items:

140) ZIPI PROTOCOL INFO           ARTI  DEC-94  MASTERMIX
133) GENERAL MIDI PATCH NAMES     PROG  MAY-94  RANDYSTACK
132) GENERAL MIDI DRUM MAP        PROG  MAY-94  RANDYSTACK
131) BIOMUSE                      ARTI  NOV-93  TRASHART
128) VIRTUAL REALITY RESEARCH     DATA  AUG-93  CZEI
127) MINDSONG TECHNICAL BRIEF     PROG  JUL-93  RANDYSTACK
125) OTTO-1604 MIDI IMPLEMENTATI  TEXT  JUL-93  MACKDESIGNS
122) MIDI MICROTUNING             DATA  MAR-93  PAN
118) SY55 EDITOR (WINDOWS)        DATA  DEC-92  PAN
113) MIDI I/O ALGORITHMS          ARTI  OCT-92  PAN
112) GRANULAR SYNTHESIS CODE      DATA  OCT-92  PAN
111) MUZIKA SOURCE                TEXT  AUG-92  PAN
110) RAVEL PROGRAMMING SYSTEM     PROG  JUL-92  PAN
109) XPANDER/MATRIX 12 SYSEX      DOCU  AUG-91  RLBUGG
108) MIDI SPEC EXPLAINED          DOCU  JUN-91  JAYCHAPMAN
107) MIDIFILE LIBRARY SOURCE      PROG  APR-91  CZEI
```

Figure B.3 Performing Artists Network (PAN) Database menu and part of MIDI database

Like a lot of on-line services, there are OLRs (off line readers) available for all the popular computing platforms including both DOS and Windows versions for the PC. The PAN OLR is called Messenger and is available free of charge by downloading it from the service. The software allows you to perform most of your PAN activities when you are disconnected from the service, only 'logging on' when you need to physically transfer messages or files to/or from the service. This approach makes going on-line somewhat less expensive since it saves you money by reducing the amount you spend connected to the service, thus reducing phone and/or service charges.

For the European user, there are two main drawbacks with PAN. The first is that a lot of the messages are only relevant to the USA (not surprisingly). The other drawback is the high cost of accessing the

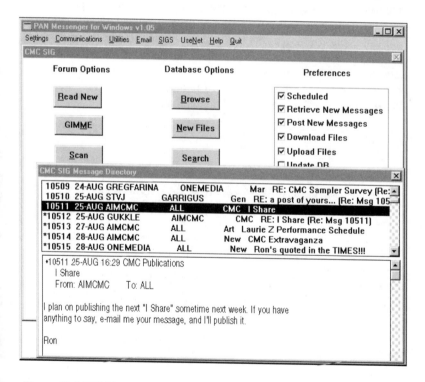

Figure B.4 PAN Messenger for Windows, a good way to keep down costs

service; you either have to dial direct across the Atlantic, get an International Packet Switch Stream (IPSS) account or access it via the Internet. Using either of the first two access methods the cost is considerable and the last is only available if you have access to an IP link.

CIX Compulink Information eXchange

CIX , which is based in London, is not specifically aimed at people in the music business (i.e. like PAN), but it does have several music areas and quite a few active musicians. CIX is set up as a number of separate conferences, each with a number of topics covering different aspects of the subject matter being discussed. For instance in the Atari ST conference (called *atari.st*), topics include ones covering MIDI (*atari.st/midi*), games (*atari.st/games*) as well as a general discussion area (*atari.st/main*) and public domain programs (*atari.st/listings*).

There are two general music areas (*music* and *route66*) and musical applications are covered in some of the machine specific areas (for instance *atari.st/midi*). There are also quite a few magazines and journalists who use the system, for instance Clive Grace who writes several music magazines (and is a Chapman Stick player to boot) is there, plus quite a few other well known names.

```
route66/music #833, from markw, 974 chars, Oct 12 21:30 95
This is a comment to message 830.
--------------------------
There's an Anatek device called a Wind Machine, but I'm afraid I don't
know what it does in detail.

I *think* you plug a BC2 into it and it produces whichever MIDI
controller you have it set to, so that you can use a BC2 with a synth
that doesn't respond to breath control, but I may be completely wrong
about that.

The WX7 has a bite sensor (as well as the wind pressure sensor), but it's
hardwired to send pitchwheel messages. There are two modes of operation,
"loose lip" and "tight lip". In loose lip the pitch bends up as you bite,
and when you aren't biting at all then there is no pitch bend. In tight
lip, you have to keep a certain amount of bite on most of the time to
keep the sensor in a dead band where there is no pitch change. If you
bite harder than this dead area the pitch bends up; if you bite less hard
than the dead zone then the pitch bends down. I've not been able to
master tight lip mode and I always use it in loose lip mode.

Mark
```

Figure B.5 CIX conference message

CIX is purely a conferencing system and doesn't provide business facilities (such as fax and telex access). It does have file databases (called flists) which allow you to download programs and data files. For instance there is a public domain sequencer in the Atari ST area and a large number of DX7 patches in the *route66* music technology area.

```
Read:flist

Filename          Size    Description
================  ======= ===============================================
column1.mid       4775    MIDI File for 1st harmony column
colmid3.zip       1024    MIDI File (zipped) for 3rd Harmony column.
sunflowr.mid      14390   Little Sunflower (chorus)
root69_m.mid      1239    Original composition to support msg # 523 (mfinger)
root69_p.mid      441     Original composition to support msg # 523 (mfinger)

Documents
~~~~~~~~~
primer.asc        248643  A rather good primer on Jazz improvisation (markw)

Utils
~~~~~
bpm.exe           23620   beats per minute program for Windows (markw)

pk361.exe         119808  The File Packer/Unpacker for unarcing all .ARC files
```

Figure B.6 CIX file list

The service covers a very large number of different topics from support areas for software companies like Borland (Turbo C and Pascal) and MicroPro (Wordstar), magazines like Amiga User, ST World and Personal Computing World, computing software and hardware and even a conference on plastic duck racing!! There are about 5,000 users on the system, and as well as local conference material, there is also a data feed from the world wide UseNet Unix conferencing system.

CIX is not connected to the public data network so that outside London you need to dial long distance, which is more expensive than PSS at peak periods. CIX does however have high speed error correcting modems which means that with either the appropriate modem or software you can spend less time on the system doing the same amount of data transfer. There are also a number of excellent OLRs available for CIX that can bring the cost of access down considerably. You can also access CIX via the Internet (see below) or ISDN.

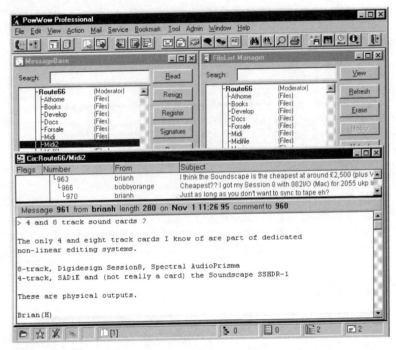

Figure B.7 PowWow, one of the many OLRs available for CIX

The Internet

One of the most confusing aspects of 'Cyberspace' is the role of the Internet. Unlike CIX and PAN which are service providers, with racks full of modems, large computers and accountants etc., the Internet is simply a standard way of connecting different computers together, just like a network. As standards go, the Internet is a pretty loose one, with everything above the basic networking protocol (which is TCP/IP) left to convention. Just looking at the plethora of buzzwords associated with the 'Net' – such as UUCP, Telnet, FTP, Gopher and the World Wide Web you can see that the whole affair is a bit of a minefield. This is usually not a problem since your service provider (say CIX) will shield you from the complexities of the Net, so I can send email to people on PAN without worrying too much about how it's done.

The Internet has a somewhat strange and chequered history. The basic concepts behind the network were devised over 30 years ago by the RAND Corporation, America's foremost Cold War think-tank, to solve the problem of communicating after a nuclear war. The basic idea is that all messages would be divided into smaller chunks (or packets). Each packet would start from a particular computer (or node) and would wind its way through the network on an individual basis. All the nodes in the network would be equal in status to all other nodes, each node with its own authority to originate, pass, and receive messages. This scheme means that if some of the computer nodes were 'down' (i.e. vaporised by an atom bomb) the message would still get through, by going 'around' the 'hole' in the network.

Although the idea originated in the US, the first network using these principles was implemented by the British National Physical Laboratory in 1968. Shortly afterwards the US Pentagon funded a project known as ARPANET which is the direct ancestor of today's Internet. Today there are tens of thousands of nodes in the Internet, scattered over the globe, with more coming on-line every day. It is

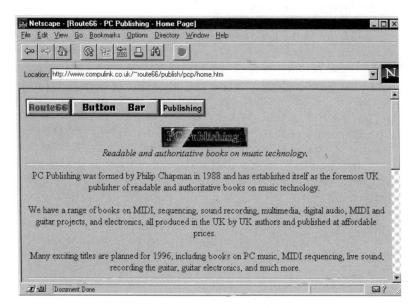

Figure B.8 The PC Publishing World Wide Web page on the CIX site

almost impossible to estimate how many people have access to the Internet, but is probably numbered in tens of millions. There are a number of ways of using the Internet, but possibly the easiest (and fastest growing method) is to use the World Wide Web. The 'web' is a hypertext based user interface that provides both a graphic interface for presenting text, graphics and multimedia elements (such as sound), and a simple 'point and click' method of navigating between nodes (or sites).

If you want to take full advantage of the facilities, your computer really has to become a 'node' on the Internet and directly access the network. There are now a large number of companies who will provide a way for you to connect into the Internet – known as Internet Service Providers. These companies usually fulfil two roles; the first is provide a way for your PC to become a node on the Internet using SLIP (Serial Line Internet Protocol) or PPP (Point to Point Protocol) via a dial-in modem connection. The second role is to provide storage space permanently connected to the Internet, so that you can have World Wide Web or FTP facilities that are available when your PC isn't actually connected to the Internet.

There ain't no such thing as a free lunch

One thing you have to realise about all these services is that they cost. In fact you have to pay twice, once to the phone company for the use of the telephone wires and then to the service provider for the use of their computers and disk drives. The costs can be kept quite low if you go on line at off peak times and try to minimise the amount of time you spend on the phone. Also the use of an off-line reader (or OLR) can reduce the time you actual spend on-line – thus accruing charges. Each service tends to have a start-up cost, a usage time charge and a minimum charge per month and prices can vary a lot so it's worth shopping around.

Appendix C
Useful addresses

This appendix contains contact addresses of companies or services mentioned in the book that might otherwise be difficult to find. The more commonplace items have been left out due to space considerations.

Akai (UK) Ltd, Haslemere Heathrow Estate, Silver Jubilee Road, Parkway, Hounslow, Middx TW4 6NQ, tel. 0181-897-6388, fax 0181-759-8268

AL Digital (CD-Grab), Voysey House, Barley Mow Passage, London W4 4PT tel: 0181-742-0755, fax: 0181-994-4959

Arbiter ProMIDI, Wilberforce Road, London NW9 6AX, tel: 0181-202-1199, fax: 0181-202-7076, Compuserve: 100315,46

Audio Design, Unit 3, Horsehoe Park, Pangbourne RG8 7JW, tel: 01734-844545, fax: 01734-842604

Boosey & Hawkes Publishing (MIDI files), The Hyde, Edgware Road, London NW9 6JN, tel: 0181-205-3861, fax: 0181-200-3737

CD Exchange, Hi-Tech House, 125 Kingswood, Norwich NR8 6UW, tel: 01603-261060, email: mm@cdex.demon.co.uk

Compulink Information eXchange, Suite 2, The Sanctuary, Oakhill Grove, Surbiton, Surrey , KT6 6DU, tel: 0181-296-9666, email: sales@cix.compulink.co.uk

Computer Music Journal, MIT Press Journals, 55 Hayward Street, Cambridge, MA 02142, USA

Creative Labs (SoundBlaster MPC soundcards), Delta House, 264 Monkmoor Road, Shrewsbury, Shropshire SY2 5ST , info:

01245-265265, tel: 01734-344322 , Technical Support - 01734-344744, BBS: 01734-360287 , Pre Sales: 01734-828291

Creative Music Coalition (computer music distribution), 1024 W. Willcox Ave, Peoria, IL 61604, USA, tel: 001-309-685-4843, fax: 001-309-685-4878, email: AIMCMC@pan.com

Demon Systems Limited (Internet provider), 42 Hendon Lane, Finchley, London N3 1TT, tel: 0181-371-1234 , fax: 0181-349-0309

Digidesign, 1360 Willow Road, #101 Menlo Park, CA 94025, USA, tel: 001-415-688-0600, 001-415-327-0777

Digital Workshop (multimedia authoring software), First Floor, 8 West Bar, Banbury, Oxon OX16 9RP, tel. 01295-258335, fax. 01295-254590

Et Cetera Distribution, Unit 15, Hardmans Business Centre, Rawtenstall, Lancs OL15 9EW, tel: 01706-228039, fax: 01706-222989, Compuserve: 100115,1616

Evolution, 8 Church Sq, Leighton Buzzard, Beds LU7 7AE, tel: 01525-372621, fax: 01525-383228

Heavenly Music (MIDI files), 39 Garden Road, Jaywick Village, Clacton, Essex CO15 2RT, tel: 01255-434217

JVC Professional Products (CD-recordable), Ullswater Hse, Kendal Ave, London W3 0XA, tel: 0181-896-6000,

Key Electronics Inc, (MIDIATOR interface), 9112 Hwy 80, W. Suite 221, Forth Worth, TX 76116, USA

Koch Media, East Street, Farnham, Surrey GU9 7XX, tel: 01252-714340, fax: 01252-711121

Korg (UK) Ltd, 8-9 The Crystal Centre, Elmgrove Road, Harrow HA1 2YR, tel: 0181-427-5377, fax: 0181-861-3595

LPA (MIDI Prolog), Logic Programming Associates, Studio 4, Royal Victoria Patriotic Building, Trinity Road, London SW18 3SX, tel: 0171-87-2016

Lyrrus Inc. (PC guitar/MIDI interface), 35 North 3rd Street, Philadelphia, PA 19106, USA, tel. 001-215-922-0880, fax. 001-215-922-7230

MayKing Records (CD-ROM production), 250 York Road, Battersea, London SW11 3SJ, tel. 0171-924-1661

MCM (PC Music Systems), MCM Building, Tudor Estate, 708a Abbey Road, London NW10 7UW, 0181-963-0663

MIDI Manufacturers' Association, P.O. Box 3173, LaHabra, CA 90632, USA, tel: 001-310-947-8689, fax: 001-310-947-4569
CompuServe, user ID: 70313,2626, e-mail address: mma@earthlink.net
Musicians' Union, National Office, 60/62 Clapham Road, London SW9 0JJ, tel: 0171-582-5566 , fax: 0171-582-9805
Music Quest Interfaces, 1700 Alma Dr, Suite 260, Plano, TX 75075, USA, tel: 001-214-881-7408
Peavey (MIDI bass guitar), Hatton House, Hunters Road, Corby, Northants NN17 5JE, tel: 01536-205520, fax: 01536-269029
PC Pro (magazine), 19 Bolsover Street, London W1P 7HJ, tel: 0171-631-1433, fax: 0171-580-6170, email: pc_pro@cix.compulink.co.uk
PC Publishing (books on music technology), Export House, 130 Vale Road, Tonbridge TN9 1SP, tel: 01732-770893 , fax: 01732-770268, email: pcp@cix.compulink.co.uk
PC Services, 40 Rowden Rd, Beckenham, Kent BR3 4NA
Roland (UK) Ltd, Atlantic Close, Swansea Enterprise Park, Swansea SA7 9FJ, tel: 01792-702701
SOS Publications Ltd (high tech music magazine), P.O. Box 30, St Ives, Cambs PE17 4XQ, tel: 01480-461244 , fax: 01480-492422
Sound Technology PLC, Letchworth Point, Letchworth, Herts SG6 1ND, tel: 01462-480000, fax: 01462-480800
Soundscape Digital Technology (hard disk recording), Crichton House, Mount Stuart Square, Cardiff Bay, Cardiff CF4 7LA, tel: 01222-450120, fax: 01222-450130
Studio Audio & Video Ltd (SADiE, hard disk recording), The Old School, Stretham, Ely, Cambs CB6 3LD, tel: 01353-648888, fax: 01353-648867
Turtle Beach Systems (MPC soundcards), P.O. Box 5074, York, Pennsylvania 17405, USA, tel: 001-717-843-6916, fax: 001-717-854-8319
Voyetra (software and interfaces), 5 Odel Plaza, Yonkers, New York, USA, NY 10701, tel: 001-914-0600
Yamaha (C1 support), Yamaha/Kemble Music (UK) Ltd, Mount Avenue, Bletchley, Milton Keynes MK1 1JE, 01908-371771

Appendix D
Suggested reading

Books
Advanced MIDI User's Guide, RA Penfold, PC Publishing
C Programming for MIDI, Jim Conger, M&T
The Compact Guide to MIDI Software for the IBM PC/PS,
Amsco
Computers and Music, RA Penfold, PC Publishing
Computer Music Projects, RA Penfold
Dirk Gently's Holistic Detective Agency, Douglas Adams, Pan
Electronic Music and MIDI Projects, RA Penfold, PC Publishing
Introducing Digital Audio, Ian Sinclair, PC Publishing
The MIDI Book, Steve De Furia and Joe Scacciaferro
The MIDI Implementation Book, Steve De Furia and Joe
Scacciaferro
MIDI for Musicians, Craig Anderton, Amsco
The MIDI Resource Book, Steve De Furia and Joe Scacciaferro
MIDI Sequencing in C, Jim Conger, M&T
MIDI Survival Guide, Vic Lennard, PC Publishing
The MIDI System Exclusive Book, Steve De Furia
MIDI, The Ins, Outs and Thrus, Jeff Rona
Mind over MIDI, Dominic Milano
Multimedia on the PC, Ian Sinclair, PC Publishing
Music Technology Reference Book, Peter Buick and Vic
Lennard, PC Publishing
Music Through MIDI, Michael Bloom
Practical MIDI Handbook, RA Penfold, PC Publishing

Principles of Digital Audio, K.C. Pohlmann, Sams
Sequencer Secrets, Ian Waugh, PC Publishing
What's MIDI?, Making Music

Reference material

Microsoft Windows Multimedia Programmer's Reference,
Microsoft Press
Microsoft Windows Multimedia Programmer's Workbook,
Microsoft Press
Microsoft Windows Multimedia Authoring and Tools Guide,
Microsoft Press
Voyetra OP4001 Programmers Manual

Magazines

Audio Media
Computer Music Journal
Electronic Musician (US)
Keyboard (US)
Future Music
PC Pro
Sound on Sound
Studio Sound
The Mix

Appendix E
Glossary

A/D, D/A Analogue to digital conversion, digital to analogue conversion.

Accidental A sharp or flat that is not part of the key signature.

Aftertouch Key pressure on a piano type keyboard, MIDI sound modules can use this information to give expression.

Application This is the software that allows you to apply your PC to a specific task, say a music system. The alternative to application software is system software which covers the operating system (ie MS/DOS) and related software (eg, GEM, Windows etc).

AT bus Another name for the Industry Standard Architecture, and is a contraction of IBM-AT expansion bus, thus compatible add-on cards are referred to as being ISA bus or AT bus cards.

Baud rate This is the usual way of describing the information capacity of a serial link (also called the bit rate). The larger the baud rate the faster the information transfer and, consequentially, the smaller the delay. The MIDI baud rate is 31,250, which means that 31,250 bits are transferred per second. Since a MIDI byte is ten bits and a MIDI message is usually three bytes we can calculate that MIDI can transfer over 1,000 musical events per second.

Bit rate Another way of saying baud rate.

Bits A bit is the smallest quantity than can be manipulated by a computer, bits are added together to get bytes which can represent numbers between 0 and 255.

Bulletin board An on-line service, usually run by a single person (the board SYSOP). These can be difficult to contact if they are popular, since they tend to have only one telephone line.

Bytes A MIDI byte is actually ten bits rather than the more normal eight, this is because two extra bits are added on to either end to allow it to be sent along a serial link. These extra bits a removed when the byte is received and only the eight data bits are used to represent the musical data.

CIX Compulink Information eXchange, a public conferencing system based in the London area, it has several music based areas.

Controller Keyboard which makes no sound itself but generates MIDI data.

DARMS Digital Alternative Representation of Musical Scores.

Data rate another way of saying baud rate.

Database An area on an on-line service or bulletin board that has data or program files in a form that you can transfer to your computer and then use. The files could contain patches for your synthesiser, sequence files or utility programs such as voice editors and the like.

DOS Disk operating system, a computer operating system loaded from disk storage (as opposed to ROM or tape based systems).

Download The process of copying a program or other data from a remote computer or an on-line service onto your computer's disk. Iinvolves using a file transfer protocol such as Kermit or Xmodem.

EBU European Broadcasting Union – they specify standards used in the broadcast industry including timecode (SMPTE/EBU) and digital audio (AES/EBU).

EPS Encapsulated PostScript.

ETLA Extended TLA (i.e. four letters) (see TLA).

Expander See sound module.

FB01 Synthesiser expander made by Yamaha.

FM Frequency modulation (technique of sound synthesis).

GEM Graphics Environment Manager, a GUI from Digital Research.

GUI Graphical user interface, this used to be called the WIMP interface (Windows, Icons, Mouse and Point) – a user interface derived from the Xerox PARC Smalltalk System, developed in the late 1970s.

IPSS International Packet Switch Stream, international version of PSS.

ISA Industry Standard Architecture, another name for the original IBM-AT expansion bus, thus compatible add-on cards are referred to as being ISA bus or AT bus cards.

IRQ Interrupt ReQuest line, used by expansion cards to 'interrupt' the PC's current task, to allow it to receive MIDI or sound data at any time, otherwise it would be missed.

Kermit A file transfer protocol developed for transferring computer files between computers. Use this to get programs and patches from the on-line service.

LA Linear arithmetic, technique of sound synthesis from Roland.

MIDI Musical Instrument Digital Interface.

MIDI file A standard format for saving a sequencer file, also referred to as SMF (Standard MIDI File). The format is an adjunct to the MIDI specification.

MOD file A file format (or module) that incorporates both sample and music data that can be replayed using a a soundcard. Also known as 'tracker' files, it was originally an Amiga format but has migrated by computer enthusiasts to most platforms including the PC (DOS and Windows).

Modem MOdulator/DEModulator, this is a box that you connect between your computer serial port and your telephone line to allow it to communicate with other computers (which must also must have a modem).

Modulation Control used to add tremolo and/or vibrato to the note played on the keyboard, a MIDI controller.

MPC Multimedia PC – the standard for audio, video and peripherals (see Appendix F).

Multitimbral The ability to play more than one sound at the same time, is used to describe an instrument (usually a synthesiser) that can produce more than one simultaneous timbre (for example a flute and a trumpet sound).

Multi-client MIDI driver This is the ability of a Windows MPC MIDI device driver to be used by more than one MIDI application, so for instance you run a synthesiser voice editor alongside your sequencer, using the same MIDI port.

Neumes Graphic symbols used for old music notation.

Online service A computer system designed to be accessed by external terminals/users, usually connected via the telephone network (PSTN).

PAN Network Originally the Performing Artists Network, a network for musicians and music biz types. Based in USA but has an international following.

Patch See voice.

Pitch bend Control used to alter the pitch of the note played on the keyboard, a MIDI controller.

Polyphony Term used to indicate the maximum number of notes that can be simultaneously played by an instrument.

Postscript Page description language.

PPQN Pulses per quarter note. The resolution of a sequencer.

Protocol The definition of the order and type of data that is transmitted on a serial line, MIDI is a serial data protocol.

PSS Packet Switch Stream, this is BT's Public Data Network (PDN) and is a computer equivalent to the PSTN.

PSTN Public Switched Telephone Network, run in the UK by British Telecom (BT) and Mercury Communications.

Quantisation Alignment of notes to coincide with beats or fractions of beats.

RAM Random access memory.

Real-time Notes are entered to a metronome, and rhythmic values are recorded.

ROM Read only memory.

Rubato The 'give and take' in the tempo of a performance.

Sampling Technique of converting an analogue sound to digital form by 'sampling' the waveform at different times.

Sequencer Program to record and play back MIDI data in real time.

Serial data Binary data sent down a single wire, one bit at a time.

SMPTE Society of Motion Picture and Television Engineers, they devised a scheme to synchronise sound to picture which is now used a lot in the music business.

Sonata font Postscript music font produced by Adobe.

Sound module or expander is essentially a synthesiser without a keyboard, the only way that these can be controlled is via MIDI. Sometimes referred to as an expansion module or rack.

Step-time Method whereby notes are entered from MIDI one by one, without rhythmic value.

Switcher this is a DOS extender that allows you to access multiple applications. Only one program is actually running at any one time, the others being stored on disk or in extended memory.

SYSOP SYStem OPerator, the person who looks after a bulletin board.

TIFF Tagged image format file.

Timbre Quality or tone-colour of a sound. Timbre is how we distinguish the difference between the same note played by two different instruments.

Timecode A signal that can be recorded onto tape that uniqely defines the location of each part of the music in terms of time (hours, minutes, seconds, frames), it derives from the film and video world.

TLA Three letter abbreviation, used a lot in computer books.

Track Area for recording in a sequencer where data is kept separate from other data.

Tracker MOD file editor (see above).

Trill Musical ornament.

TSR Terminate and stay resident program (like Borland's SideKick). These 'pop up' programs can effectively give you multi-tasking, since you don't need to exit the program you are running to use them. The downside is that they take up system memory (ie RAM) whether you use them or not. An alternative to TSRs is to use a DOS switcher programme like Software Carousel.

Turn Musical ornament.

UART Universal asynchronous receiver/transmitter.

Upload The process of copying a program or other data from your computer to a distant computer or an on-line service using a modem. The process involves using a file transfer protocol such as Kermit or Xmodem.

Velocity The speed (or how hard) the keys on a piano keyboard are hit, used to derive the loudness of the note.

Voice the parameters of the sound generators of a synthesiser that defines the sound (or timbre) produced by the synthesiser electronics. Synths usually have a number of internal memories that store these parameters, these can be selected via MIDI.

Windows A GUI operating system/environment from from Microsoft, current variants include Windows 3.1, Windows for Workgroups 3.11, Windows 95 and Windows NT.

Xmodem Like Kermit but different.

Ymodem Another file download format, faster than Xmodem.

Zmodem Latest file download protocol derived from Xmodem.

Appendix F
The Multimedia PC Specification

MPC 1 – The Multimedia Specification Level 1

The level 1 specification is as follows:

- A 386SX microprocessor with 2 MB of RAM
- A 3.5-inch high-density floppy disk drive
- A hard disk drive with at least 30 MB of disk space
- A colour monitor with 640 by 480 pixels with 16 colours
- A 2-button mouse
- System software that offers binary compatibility with the Microsoft Windows operating system version 3.0 with Multimedia extensions

A CD-ROM drive that meets the following criteria:

- A sustained data transfer rate of 150 kilobytes per second
- A CPU bandwidth usage of 40 percent or less when maintaining a sustained data transfer rate of 150 kilobytes per second
- An average seek time of 1 second or less

Audio subsystem that includes the following items:

- An 8-bit digital-to-analogue converter (DAC) capable of processing waveform-audio files recorded at 22.05 and 11.025 kHz sampling rates
- An 8-bit analogue-to-digital converter (ADC) capable of recording waveform-audio files at the sample rate of 11.025 kHz through an external source, such as a microphone

- Internal synthesiser capabilities with four or nine multivoice, multitimbral capacity, and two simultaneous percussive notes

MPC 2 – The Multimedia Specification Level 2

The level 2 specification is:

- A 25 Mhz 486SX microprocessor with 4 MB of RAM
- A 3.5-inch high-density floppy disk drive
- A hard disk drive with at least 160 MB of disk space
- A 101-key keyboard with a standard DIN connector or one that provides identical functionality by using key-combinations
- A two-button mouse with a serial or bus connector
- A MIDI (Musical Instrument Digital Interface) port that includes MIDI OUT, MIDI IN, and MIDI THRU, and that has interrupt support for input and FIFO transfer
- An IBM-style analogue or digital joystick (game) port
- A colour monitor with a display resolution of 640 by 480 pixels with 65,536 colours
- System software that offers binary compatibility with Windows 3.0 with Multimedia Extensions or Windows 3.1

A CD-ROM drive that meets the following criteria:

- A sustained data transfer rate of 300 kilobytes per second
- A CPU bandwidth usage of 40 percent or less when maintaining a sustained data transfer rate of 150 kilobytes per second, or a CPU bandwidth of 60 percent or less when maintaining a sustained data transfer rate of 300 kilobytes per second
- An average seek time of 400 milliseconds or less
- A 10,000 hour mean-time-between-failures rating
- CD-ROM XA ready (mode 1 capable, mode 2 form 1 capable, mode form 2 capable)
- Multisession capable
- MSCDEX-2.2 driver or equivalent that implements the extended audio functions

An audio subsystem that includes the following items:

- A CD-ROM driver with CD-DA (Red Book audio) outputs and volume control

A 16-bit DAC with the following characteristics:

- Linear PCM (Pulse Code Modulation) sampling
- DMA or FIFO buffered transfer capability with interrupt on buffer empty
- Mandatory sample rates of 44.1, 22.05, and 11.025 kHz
- Stereo channels
- CPU bandwidth usage of 10 percent or less when outputting audio of 22.05 or 11.025 kHz sample rate, or a CPU bandwidth of 15 percent or less when outputting audio of 44.1 kHz sample rate

A 16-bit ADC with the following characteristics:

- Linear PCM sampling
- DMA or FIFO buffered transfer capability with interrupt on buffer empty
- Mandatory sample rates of 44.1, 22.05, and 11.025 kHz
- Microphone input
- Internal synthesiser capabilities with multivoice, multitimbral, six simultaneous melody notes plus two simultaneous percussive notes

Internal mixing with the following capabilities:

- Can combine three audio sources and present the output as a stereo, line-level audio signal at the back panel
- Mixing sources are CD Red Book audio, synthesiser, and DAC
- Each mixing source has 3-bit volume control with a logarithmic taper

Index

PC Music Handbook